TELLS OF A SOUTHERN BOY
Precious Memories

PAUL "BUSTER" TURNER

outskirts
press

Table of Contents

Foreword

My first book, *Tells of a Southern Boy: A Life in Stories*, was not going to be a book, but a collection of stories that my son, Paul M. Turner III, wanted written. He wanted them recorded so that our ancestors would enjoy these stories. Because our extended family and friends also wanted to read this collection of memories, the book was developed and became a reality. Several hundred people have read the book and their comments have been very satisfying. My one regret with the first book was that the editing was not what it should have been. I had to learn the hard way that self-editing is not a good idea. As the one doing the writing, you can't see the trees for the forest. This is particularly true if you weren't an English major.

My second book, *Tells of a Southern Boy: Precious Memories*, was written because one memory leads to another memory. The brain is a complex computer and once a vault from a period of your life is opened, then many memories outpour that were stored and dormant. The new book will capture many experiences, events, and people that shaped, my wife, Jane's and my life. This book is more serious than my first book. Stories are mostly about family, friends, professional associates, and events that impacted our lives. *Tells of a Southern Boy: Precious Memories* has been edited by my friend and classmate, David Smoak. Therefore, most edits have been caught this time and changed accordingly.

As with the first book, *Tells of Southern Boy: Precious Memories* encompasses stories (memories) over several decades. Therefore, the spelling of names and places, time lines, and the actual events as they are remembered may not be 100% correct. This was not intentional, but hopefully will be forgiven. At no time did I write anything to embarrass anyone. As with my first book, I try to be real and even state things about myself that are true and sometimes embarrassing. However, all events, good and bad, shape our character and our life. As I age, I am happy about my life and the time in which I was raised. I am proud of my family and their accomplishments. I appreciate the people that have passed through my life and the impact they have made. Most of all I am thankful that God gave me my memories and an opportunity to share them with others. With all that I stated above, I hope you enjoy the last of the books sharing my memories.

Paul and Jane

Jane and I have been married for more than 59 years. Therefore, we have done many things together, have observed numerous events and happenings, and have known many friends and personalities during our life. This section covers the stories on the exciting road of life.

Arden Elementary: A Community Treasure

Johnny Bloodworth recently mentioned me in a Facebook post by Gene Lee concerning Arden Elementary School and the principal, Pearl Harvey. We called her Ms. Harvey. She ruled with a firm hand and corporal punishment was accepted and applauded by the parents in the community. In fact, without question, if I had earned a spanking at school, I would have gotten a second spanking at home. I remember a fellow classmate, Johnny Mills, committed an infraction that resulted in a whipping by Ms. Harvey with a thick yardstick. I can assure you it was a real spanking. You could hear the whacks from the cloakroom. Ms. Harvey had taught my daddy, his sister, Pearl Doris, and his brother, Gene. As a result, although certainly not a perfect student, I remained vigilant not to have a major offense that required the wrath of Ms. Harvey. As Iris Windham mentioned in the same Facebook post, the country would greatly benefit from the same firm, but fair, discipline today.

With the communication by Gene, Johnny, and Iris Windham, the memories of Arden Elementary School and the College Place community came flooding back. First, Johnny's mother, Shirley, was my den mother when I was in the Cub Scouts. She was always one of my favorites. Later, we were destined to work together at the South Carolina Board of Health. Her son, Johnny, did too. The Bloodworth family were neighbors and went to College Place Methodist Church with my family. Gene Lee's father and my father had worked for bakeries as did another classmate's, Jeff Flanders, daddy. Our community was special and after all these years, many of us are still connected no matter where we live.

Arden Elementary was a pillar in the community and had a strong Parent, Teacher Association (PTA). Many events were hosted by the school during the different seasons of the year. The playground was used by all the children in the community. I remember routine basketball, football, and baseball games. At times, there would be children all over the grounds playing different marble games. At other times, yo-yo games would be center stage. We would congregate, pick teams, and play for hours. I can't remember everyone, but I do remember my cousins, Roy and Johnny Neville, Jack and Jake Halford, Robert and Don McMillian, Martin Lightsey, Buddy Robinson, Thomas Ray, Hiram Allen, Johnny Goodale, Ronnie Barker, Johnny Bloodworth, and Bobby Haynes. There were many others that played with us at one time or another, but after all these years, I can't remember their names. Most of these people went on to play one or more high school sports. At least three of these individuals received a college athletic scholarship: Jack Halford, Buddy Robinson, and Thomas Ray. To say that whatever sport we played at Arden was competitive would be an understatement. I remember my cousin, Johnny, and Buddy Robinson competing to see who could hit the baseball the farthest distance. Sometimes Hiram Allen would factor in on the competition. Arden school was definitely the center of our universe.

After all these years, I can still remember Johnny Neville, my cousin, and I being invited to Betty Lou Lee's birthday party. In truth Johnny was invited, but since I was with him, I was included. She was one of the prettiest and sweetest girls in our class. I believe we were in the second or third grade. On the day of the party, Johnny and I along with some others headed across Wilson Boulevard to Betty's house. To our surprise and chagrin there was no party. To this day I believe Betty Lou wanted the party so bad that she was going to make it happen. Unfortunately, her family was not in sync with her dream. I have seen Betty Lou at high school class reunions and she is always the same pretty and sweet person.

Arden Elementary and the College Place section of Eau Claire was a special place. Arden is still a functional school today, but has been remodeled and a great deal larger than when I attended. It may be of interest to some that my Granddaddy Turner was president of the school board.

Pop's General Store: Memories Galore

My Pop Boykin, Robert H. Boykin, owned and operated a large grocery store in Eau Claire. At least it seemed large to me. Compared to the chain stores that we see today, it was probably not near as big. The store was part of a large complex that included a liquor store, a barber shop, and a few other business establishments. The complex stood between a fork in the road, Monticello Road and Main Street. Pop's store had a thriving business that featured the very best meats in the area. He made his own sausage and featured cuts of meat that were outstanding. He used to get up at the break of dawn, work in his large garden, eat a hearty breakfast, and then open the store at 7:00. This happened six days a week. He would come home about noon for a sandwich and a short nap. Then he would return to the store and work to after 7:00. People worked hard and a workday was long back then. The only day off was the Sabbath. He also owned a small diner in a nearby complex that his wife, my Mimi Boykin, operated. The

3

food was southern and very good. My grandparents had a good life and enjoyed their family very much. They liked simple things, family gatherings and fishing.

One thing I learned about my granddaddy was that he learned how important a good breakfast was as a tobacco farmer in Johnston County, North Carolina. His breakfast consisted of a big pot of coffee made the old way on the stove. He always had homemade biscuits, gravy, eggs, grits, onions, and tomatoes. The meats varied, but were always abundant. One morning it would be country ham. Another morning it would be salt mackerel. The next morning it may be pork chops or fried fish. The number of calories was staggering, but worked off by hard 12-hour workdays. Lord help us today if we ate the same way.

As I got older, I helped Pop in the store. He taught me how to appropriately bag groceries. Don't make the bags too heavy. Be careful in bagging fragile items like eggs and bread. Every time I go to the store today and see someone bagging groceries, I remember what he taught me. He taught me how to stock the shelves with various items. He taught me how to sweep the wooden floors with a heavy broom using sawdust to cut down on the dust. However, what I remember most was how much work was involved in operating a grocery store. The one part of the operation that I never learned was the meat department. Because there was a great deal of risk associated in cutting, slicing, and grinding meat, Granddaddy was reluctant in teaching me in my adolescent years. When I got old enough to learn, I was playing sports. Therefore, I never learned that part of the business.

At some point Pop sold the business at the right time and made out well. It was timely as the large chain stores were becoming the future. A few years later when my Uncle Bobby Boykin dropped out of Wofford College, he wanted to reopen the grocery store with Pop.

Of course, Pop jumped at the opportunity to be in partnership with his son. Several years later the store failed. Two different families eating out of the store and competing with large grocery chains was too much. This time the venture cost him dearly. In back reflection had they gone into a specialty meat business they would probably have done extremely well. Uncle Bobby had become a very proficient butcher. He had learned well from Pop. Bobby as a professional butcher worked for years in the Irmo area.

I found out after starting to date Jane Miller, now my wife, that her mother, Lavinia Corley Miller, used my Pop's store on a regular basis. She favored the store because of its variety of products, especially his meats. She shopped there for her grocery needs for the home economics department at the high school which she chaired. She also shopped there because her husband who grew up in the country liked the same foods that my grandfather enjoyed. He had abundance of these foods in his store. Jane later told me that Pop showed her the first hundred-dollar bill that she had ever seen.

One side story concerns the barbershop that was behind Granddaddy's grocery store. The two barbers, Tom and Chavis, were always playing pranks on me. They would tell me to ask my Pop to send them a pound of chicken teeth. Another time, they needed a pound of chicken feet. I always took them at their word and was the centerpiece for their amusement. One day Chavis asked me to go get a pound of mothballs. I had enough and told him there was no such thing as mothballs. Yep, they laughed so hard that they had tears in their eyes.

For several years Pop, in addition to his heavy load with the grocery store and diner, was also a councilman and at one time Vice-Mayor of Eau Claire.

Good memories of a good man that I loved with all my heart and still miss today.

Helping My Daddy at Claussen's Bakery

My daddy, Paul M. Turner, was one of the managers at Claussen's Bakery. His title was route supervisor which meant he supervised several employees that ran bread routes. As a supervisor he ran various routes when his men were on vacation or sick. At times he took me to help him. Most of the time, this was on Saturday or during the summer when I was out of school. For the most part I enjoyed being with him and being introduced to his customers. Many of the customers were also his friends. Daddy had a personality that made him bond with most people quickly. This was evident when he passed away at 80 years of age. The church was packed with some attendees actually standing in the rear of the church. This was very unique for he was a common man without any regal achievements, not a politician, and had no grand title. However, his life had touched many people and had made many better for having known him. All this being said, his customers treated me nice and their warmth was genuine.

I learned many things from working with my father. First, he worked long hours and the work was hard. Serving many customers in one day was a challenge. We left the house at about 4:30. Then we loaded the truck. He left bread at the first stops at their door because they had not opened yet. He would stop back by these stores on the way back to the bakery. He always had a special place selected for breakfast. We normally had breakfast at about 7:00. The same thing applied for lunch which was about 12:30. At each stop, he would check the order, load the order while in the truck. He then would deliver the order. He would also check the items on the shelves to make sure that they were not expired. Expired items would be replaced with fresh items at no charge to the customer. This same process happened stop after stop. At the end of the route, we would head back to the bakery stopping at several places on the way. Once back at the bakery, the truck would be unloaded with an accounting of all products left on the truck at the end of the day. Then he had to count all the money collected, the returned items, and the unsold items. We usually got home about 6:30, sometimes later. This was a long day and this was done by his route men six days a week. Tell me that people didn't work hard in the 1950s.

I remember several other things while working with Dad. The trucks were metal and had no air conditioners back then. In the summer even with the doors open, the truck was very hot and miserable. All my clothes were dripping wet. I learned why my daddy was completely drained at the end of the day. Many nights, he would lie down on the bed and go sound asleep before eating supper. I learned and appreciated what my father did to support his family. I learned why he wanted me to do better than he had done. He wanted me to get a college education. Since I loved him and wanted to be with him, I endured some of what he did on most days. The few dollars he paid me, the meals I ate, and the pastries I enjoyed were not enough to make me want to work for a bakery to make a living.

Kids Will Be Kids

One night my girlfriend, Jane, and I were double dating with Hank Garrison and his date, Margy Oppenlander. We were in Hank's daddy's new Lincoln Continental. It was a big luxury car with all the bells and whistles. I remember that I was impressed with the rear window that would open and the regal spare tire that was covered, mounted, and very visible from the rear of the car. I remember feeling very special as we cruised through our favorite drive-ins, Sewell's and the Varsity. It would really be special if all our schoolmates would take notice. I don't remember everything we did on that evening, but we must have become bored. The decision was made by three of us with Hank the driving force to toilet paper some teachers' yards. The lone negative vote was Jane. Since her mother, Lavinia Miller, was a teacher at our high school, Eau Claire, she wanted no part in the endeavor. In order to accomplish our dastardly deed, we had to select the teachers who would receive our attention. Believe it or not, we selected teachers based on who we liked and because they lived close by. An additional element to the selection was that we had to know where they lived. The two selected were Hester Berry and Carolyn Lucas.

After purchasing several rolls of toilet paper, we headed toward our targets. The first home that we reached was Carolyn Lucas's. Hank, Margy, and I crept toward the yard. Jane wasn't going to be involved. The three of us entered the yard and for what seemed a very longtime spread toilet paper on the shrubs and on every tree in the yard. By throwing toilet rolls up into the trees, paper was hanging from the highest branches. By the time we got through, it looked like it had snowed paper. It was a masterful job. With our mission complete, we snuck back to the car. Then we headed to Ms. Berry's home and worked feverishly to complete our last event. Satisfied, the three of us headed back to the car. We hoped no one had seen or recognized us. Once in the car, we drove past both homes to inspect our handiwork. We had done a marvelous job.

We told absolutely no one about what we had done. However, the word had gotten out about papering the two homes. It was the talk around the school. There were four people who knew, but they weren't about to tell. Every time I walked past Ms. Lucas and Ms. Berry, I felt like they knew something. Years later as an adult I had my yard papered and I didn't think it was so funny. Kids will be kids.

You Better Not Make Me Mad

My cousin, Roy Neville, and I played together on the Eau Claire High School Shamrocks football team. Roy was a year ahead of me in high school. He was a very good player even though he was not a real big player. His senior year he was captain of the Shamrocks and made first team center on the All-Area team. It is no doubt in my mind that if he had been bigger and taller, he would have received a scholarship to play college football somewhere. He was also president of his high school class. Therefore, he was a leader off and on the field.

Roy and I were both competitive players and in practice sometimes we butted heads. For some reason, I don't remember now what, he made me mad. If we were playing on opposite sides of the ball, I would find Roy and hit him as hard as I could. Since I outweighed him by 40 pounds, he was taking a licking. After a while he was no longer concerned about his blocking or tackling assignment. All he was worried about was where I was. I really don't know why the coach let this occur, but he never stopped me. Maybe he was making Roy tougher. At the end of practice, he was worn out.

Why I remember this after all these years, I really don't know. What I do know is that when I was mad, I played with a great deal more intensity. If I could have played mad all the time, I would have been a better football player. I loved Roy like a brother then and I love Roy like a brother today.

The Best Eggnog Ever

When we lived on Holmes Avenue in the College Place section of Eau Claire, I remember vividly a unique visit from my Granddaddy Turner, Paul Crawford Turner. My mother and daddy were entertaining my Granddaddy Boykin and my great uncle, Burnie Goldson. My mother had made from scratch a big bowl of eggnog. She had used bourbon to cook the eggs. In other words, the eggnog included an ample amount of alcohol. The reason for Grandaddy Boykin and Uncle Burnie's visit was to imbibe in Mother's delicious Christmas cheer. They had one cup and Mother was ladling out the second cup when the front door bell rang. It was Grandaddy Turner. His visit was treated with warmth and anxiety at the same time. You might ask why the anxiety? He was a staunch Southern Baptist and he was totally opposed to alcohol in any way, shape, or form. He would not even take medicine if it included alcohol. Grandaddy was so respected that my daddy and my Uncle Gene, a World War II veteran, would not get anywhere near him if they were drinking. In fact, when I became an adult and had a drink, I wouldn't get within a block of his house.

With this background, Grandaddy Turner asked what they were having to drink. When he was told it was Mother's homemade eggnog, his refrain was, "I love eggnog." Of course, he was referring to eggnog without enhancement. Mother had little choice but to go get him a glass of eggnog. He enjoyed it so much that he asked for a second. He certainly enjoyed the eggnog and the company. As he got up to leave, he told Mother that was the best eggnog he had ever had. It was a very sincere compliment. To my knowledge, he never knew he had consumed alcohol. I wonder if that might be the reason it was the best eggnog ever.

A side story, I loved eggnog too. I could consume a great deal at one sitting. Mother on another occasion had made homemade eggnog. After a get-together, she left the remaining eggnog in the refrigerator. It was in a quart milk bottle. When I got home from school, I found the bottle and devoured it. Yes, it contained alcohol. Boy, what a tongue-lashing I received when she got home. The trials and tribulations of drinking eggnog.

One of the Best Blocks Ever

During my junior year in high school, our Eau Claire High School football team played an away game with Bishopville. School buses were loaded with the football team, band, and cheerleaders. Then we all headed in a convoy followed by parents and fans. Away games were always exciting and stressful at the same time. Playing football on a strange field and a hostile crowd is challenging. However, our team under our new head coach, Art Baker, and his staff were playing at a level way beyond what had ever been done in the past. Expectations by the team and the community were high and we as a team expected to be competitive in every game whether we were playing at home field, Memorial Stadium, or away.

Soon after the game started Bishopville kicked to us. Dewain Herring was back to field the kick. Several of us linemen made a wall or corridor as we had been trained. Dewain made his way behind the wall and headed down the field. My cousin, Roy Neville, was the first lineman that Bishopville team tried to breach to get to our back. Roy threw a flying block and literally took three Bishopville players down. It was one of the most spectacular blocks I had ever seen. Buddy Robinson blocked another player and I successfully blocked another player. With these blocks being made, Dewain was off to the end zone for a touchdown. In communicating with Dewain about this play, he said Roy and the rest of us protected his scrawny posterior. Eau Claire won the game 21 to 7. This would be the first winning season in Eau Claire's history. This would be the precursor to the 1960 team that would be arguably best football team ever.

A sad side note concerning the life of Dewain Herring follows. He was President of his Class and graduated with honors. He graduated from the University of South Carolina with an undergraduate degree and a law degree. He had a very successful law practice and was selected one year as the most outstanding lawyer in Columbia. One night after a day of golf that included drinking, he went to a strip joint for relaxation and more drinks. He had an altercation with management over something he was doing and he was thrown out of the club. I might add that I have heard that he was bipolar and on medications. These medications and alcohol should not be used together. He proceeded to his car and as he passed the front door, he fired his pistol. Unfortunately, the bouncer who was behind the door, was killed. After a long trial, Dewain was convicted of murder and given a life in prison. The fact that he was a lawyer and should have known better and other implications concerning the judge resulted, in my opinion, a very unreasonable sentence. Premeditated murders and gang-related killings have resulted in far less sentences. There have been several appeals with no positive results. I still communicate regularly with him and if his sentence is not reduced, he will be released at age 94. A bad mistake by a good man has resulted in a destroyed life. The one thing that is very much a positive: Dewain is very sorry for what he did, has asked forgiveness, and knows Jesus Christ as his Lord and Savior. He is now in a prison for seniors in Pelzer that is by far his safest environment ever while being in the South Carolina penal system.

Green and White Fight, Black and White Fight

In the late 1950s there were football games going on at Eau Claire High School that were unsanctioned. Initially, pickup football games among present and former football players were played most weekends. Of course, there was no football uniforms and pads that are usually associated with playing football. The games were intense and they definitely were not touch football. The tackling and blocking were full-bore and at the end of every game there were casualties. Some of the injuries at times were significant. I am not sure what the consequences would have been if our coaches had found out about these games. The current Eau Claire High School football players would have been, at a minimum, instructed to immediately desist. Over time, black athletes from the surrounding neighbor gathered to watch the games. At some point, the black athletes were included in the games. Eventually, the black athletes formed their own team. Competition between the white and black athletes was very competitive and both sides performed at high levels. Team leaders made sure the games were fair and that nothing dirty or unfair occurred. The play was intense and both sides gave everything to win. Some of the hitting was ferocious. Both teams featured some outstanding athletes and would forecast outstanding Eau Claire sports teams in the future when the high school became integrated. Eau Claire's school colors were green and white. Therefore, "Green and White Fight" was one of our cheers. On the weekend, games were black and white fight with the best team winning.

In the 1950s and 1960s change was coming. Although our parents didn't want it, my generation didn't understand it, but we recognized it was coming. Young people of all races are the same. A sport like football brought two different races together for the love of the game. Sports broke down barriers at Eau Claire High School.

We Won the Game in Every Aspect

One of the first football games my senior year that really demonstrated that Eau Claire High School had a powerhouse team to be reckoned with was when we played Brooklyn-Cayce (BC). The Bearcat team featured a running back, Mike Derrick, that was truly one of the best overall athletes in South Carolina. Mike would be eventually become a professional baseball player and perform in some games in the Major Leagues. This clearly illustrates his superior athletic ability. Mike's daddy, Jimmy, and my daddy played golf together regularly at Lexington Country Club. It should also be noted, another one of our premier player's, Larry Sharpe, Daddy, GL, was also a member of the foursome. Buddy Robinson and some of our players played American Legion Baseball with Mike and some of the other BC athletes. This is an around about way of showing that many of our players had a relation with some of the Brooklyn-Cayce players.

On the week before our game with Brooklyn-Cayce, our head football coach, Art Baker, came into the locker room and threw the sports section of The State newspaper on a bench and left. One of our team members picked the paper up and read it. He was horrified at what he read and announced that the prediction was for Mike Derrick and Company to rout Eau Claire. To put it very mildly, we as a team were not very happy with the prediction. All the senior leadership on our team made it our goal to show the newspaper and the community what we were made of.

From the time the football game started to the game ended, the Eau Claire team dominated the game. Our offensive line opened up big holes in the BC line and our backs ran all over them. When they adjusted to shut down our running attack, our quarterback, Thomas Ray, shredded their secondary with accurate passes. Our defense completely shut down Mike Derrick and their powerful offense. At the end of the day, Eau Claire beat Brooklyn-Cayce 30-7.

A few memories from the game that are still vivid to me after all these years. They had a big tackle, Wilbur Fallaw. He would eventually earn a football scholarship to play for the Citadel. It was my luck to draw him as my opponent on offense and defense. He outweighed me by at least 50 pounds. In talking to my line coach, Steve Robertson, I asked how I best handle such a large adversary. His answered that I should aim at his crotch. Once the game started I did exactly what I had been directed. When we had the ball, my block would always be directed toward Wibby's crotch. It worked like a charm. By the end of the first quarter, before I could get to him, he was backing up. Obviously, the coach used this situation on more than one occasion to move the ball down the field.

On one defensive play, Mike Derrick ran off the end of the line and to my horror he was coming right toward me. I remembered what I had been taught, keep your eyes glued to his midriff and totally disregard whatever other moves are made. He twisted, juked, and made other assorted moves which were designed to make me commit. I kept my eyes on his belt region. The only move left for Mike was to jump over me. As he leaped, I caught one foot and he came tumbling down. When I got up and looked behind me, I saw nothing but clear sailing. If I hadn't made the tackle, he would have scored. I know to this day, if I had known that there was no one behind me, I would have missed the tackle.

I just heard another story about the game from Billy Ward, one of our captains. Buddy Robinson was our defensive captain, and as such he called the defense alignments and the plays. According to Billy, Buddy called a play where Buddy as a tackle would blitz and Billy as a linebacker would fill in the hole in the line left by Buddy. It worked to perfection. Buddy went in unimpeded and hit Mike Derrick with everything he had. Mike certainly felt the lick. Per Mike Derrick, at halftime the BC coach was trying to fire up his team and said Eau Claire was really not hitting that hard. Whereby Mike said without hesitation, Coach they are knocking the stew out of us on every play, or something to that effect.

The team that was to be routed did the routing.

Protect Our Colors at Any Cost

In my junior year at Eau Claire High School, both our boys' basketball team and our girls' basketball teams were by far the best in school history. Both the teams won the South Carolina AA Basketball Championships. As a result, our student body supported both teams at home games and when they were on the road. I recollect a couple stories that concerned out-of-town games.

At the Dentsville game, I remember Will Bruce Bush telling us that at some point he was going to capture their mascot. I don't remember what the creature was, but their cheerleaders had it in their possession. At some point at the end of the game, he made good on his promise. The mascot was taken by Will Bruce and out the door of the gym he went with the mascot. The male part of Dentsville's student body went out the door chasing him. This made it interesting for Will Bruce and any Eau Claire student that was wearing a Shamrock letter jacket or sweater. He got roughed up and my cousin, Roy Neville, and several others got in fights protecting Will. I was not in the immediate area where the main fighting had occurred, but I was soon surrounded by a number of Dentsville fans that were becoming aggressive. I knew I was going at a minimum to get beat up. As they were getting ready to attack and I do mean attack, a voice from the rear of the group said, "This is Buster Turner, he is a nice guy, leave him alone." It was one of their football players that I had scrimmaged against before the football season started. Thanks to him I was spared a thrashing. Since I was riding with Roy, I had to find his

15

car. When I got to the car, Roy and Will Bruce were already there and both showed visible effects from their encounter. Roy was still mad at the Dentsville students. Had it been the reverse, Eau Claire students would have done the same thing. I believe I was more upset with Will Bruce for doing something stupid.

At another road game, our boys' basketball team was playing Carlisle Military School in Camden. After the game, as our team was heading back to the bus, one of our younger players, Bobby Cole, was being shoved around by some cadets. Buddy Robinson, John Knight, and I were riding together. On seeing what was happening, we jumped out of the car to defend him. Buddy immediately took on the largest cadet and fought him until he backed off. John literally flew into the group and as he passed me, he handed me a wooden-metal filled baton. This literally prevented me from becoming involved in the fight. What was I going to do with the baton that I had no intention of using? John didn't want to use it and I sure wasn't going to use it. I always regretted not participating in the fight to protect our players and our colors. But on reflection, maybe it was good thing that I had the baton. After several minutes, the aggressive cadets started to disband for two reasons. First, their leaders were getting their butts beat. Secondly, adult school leaders could be seen coming our way. Recently, Bobby Cole told some of us that he was glad we were nearby. He was sure that he had a big problem on his hands and our intervention on his behalf was appreciated. Bobby, because of his outstanding play in high school, received a football scholarship from the University of South Carolina and was a great player.

Dedicated and Tough as Nails

In high school I was privileged to play football with some great athletes. In my senior year three members in my class were special players. Thomas Ray, Buddy Robinson, and Billy Ward were all exceptional players and our team captains. They were the nucleus for what I think was the best football team in Eau Claire High School history. Thomas was our All-State quarterback. Buddy was our All-State tackle, and Billy was our All-State fullback. All three went to the Shrine Bowl game which is composed of the best football players from South and North Carolina. All three received football scholarships to Clemson.

Of these three players, Billy Ward was without question the most dedicated and had the most heart. Billy gave 100% on each play. You could always count on him to make his block on every play. At Clemson he received the Atlantic Coast Conference Jacobs Blocking Trophy Award which signified he was the best blocker in the conference. If we needed yards for a first down, we could count on him to gain the yards. To illustrate how dedicated Billy was, at one practice he dislocated his shoulder and he had to be taken to get medical attention. After the shoulder was reset, Bill came back to practice and finished with the rest of us. This illustrated how tough he was. In talking to Charles O'Brian, the guard who played by me on both sides of the ball for two years, we both agreed that no one else on the team would have done what Billy did. In fact, I knew a player or two among the starters that would have milked the injury to miss practice for a day or two.

Billy's dedication to his studies in college paid off big-time. After getting his degree at Clemson, he received a Doctor of Philosophy from Michigan in what I believe was Agriculture Economics. He had a successful career with the World Bank, his own consulting firm, and as a Clemson professor. At Clemson he was made Professor Emeritus. Billy epitomizes the statement about making the best out of what God gives you.

It is with sadness that after I wrote the above article about Dr. William Ward that he passed away. In one of my last conversations with him, he made a couple of revelations. He told me that if he hadn't received the scholarship to play football at Clemson, he wouldn't have been able to attend college. His parents couldn't have afforded it. He also stated how proud he was that his agriculture economics had made a difference in countries and people's lives all over the world. Without question my football mate, classmate, and friend made a difference. May he rest in peace.

High Schoolmates That Were Good Role Models

There are always older students in high school that influence your life. Most of these students have no idea how they impact the lives of others. This also applies to what we do and how the way in which we do it affects other people. The Eau Claire High School upper-class members that had effect on my life in alphabetical order are: Edith Denniston, Ted Fetner, Linda Holland, Preston Irby, Roy Neville, and Buddy Sharpe. I might mention that four of these individuals went to church with me and my family. The one trait that was common to all of them was that they had a special gift from God, but the way they treated others was very unique. I learned from each of these schoolmates that the way we treat others has a profound effect on peoples' lives. I know it did in my life. They treated everyone the same way. I will discuss each one below.

Edith Denniston was a beautiful person inside and out. She was head cheerleader, a class officer, Miss D.A.R., senior superlative (most school spirit), and the list goes on and on. She was special in numerous ways, but the most special thing about Edith was that she always treated everybody the same way. She never let her accolades put her on a pedestal. I observed this by being around her at College Place Methodist Church and during junior high school and high school. What you see is what you get. That was true then and it is true now. She married a schoolmate, Danny Varn, who has the same trait. They still live in the Columbia metropolitan area.

Ted Fetner was captain of the football team, class president, senior superlatives (best-looking and best-athlete), and was involved in many more activities. He was definitely a school leader and role model for many. Ted was certainly a role model for me. He was enjoyable to be around and never was haughty or had an attitude that he was better than anyone else. To illustrate his personality, when I stayed with my Pop and Mimi Boykin, he would come by and pick this underclassman up and haul me back and forth to football practice. Ted graduated from South Carolina in chemical engineering and married his high school sweetheart, Wynnette Prince. They now have homes in Pennsylvania and the Columbia area and go back and forth. A very sad note to add to this story, I just found out that Ted recently succumbed to cancer. Another good man is no longer with us.

Linda Holland was another beautiful person who was very popular. She was a cheerleader, was selected Miss Junior and Homecoming Queen, and voted the senior superlative (friendliest and best all-around). She was heavily involved in many other school activities. Without question, she really was one of the friendliest students at Eau Claire High School. Our families went to College Place Methodist Church together. My observation was that Linda's personality was the same wherever she was. She was indeed one of the best of the best. She was one of the people that certainly taught me what is most important in life.

Preston Irby was a quite leader that became friends with me in elementary school. He was serious and funny too. Although he was few years older, he had no problems hanging out with me. Since we were neighbors, there was many a night that we watched television programs at his home. Preston's family also went to College Place Methodist with mine. I remember when he got his EC letter for playing track, he placed it on a magnificent off-white sweater instead of the traditional green and white jacket. His sweater served as my motivation to play high school sports. I wanted an EC letter. Preston graduated from the University of South Carolina and later received his dental degree. He practiced dentistry for years in the Charleston area. He married another schoolmate, Patsy Hinnant, who attended church with us.

Roy Neville and his brother, Johnny were my cousins and really were like my brothers. Roy being the oldest of the three of us served as a model for Johnny and me. What Roy did, we wanted to do the same. Because he played football, then I wanted to play football. We were always very competitive in anything that we were involved. Roy was president of his class, captain of the football team, received the senior superlatives (friendliest and most school spirit), and the list goes on and on. Roy graduated from University of South Carolina and had an outstanding career in pharmaceutical sales, being selected on more than one occasion as being the best in the nation. He met Charlotte Orr in college and they have been successfully married for decades. Roy made a difference in my life and after all these years, we are still very close.

Buddy Sharpe and his family went to College Place Methodist church with me and my family. I played football with Buddy and even rode to football practice with him and a couple other players. Although Buddy was a couple of years older than I was and was one of Eau Claire's best athletes, he treated everyone like they had value. Buddy was the same way at church. He carried me and others to various church activities and events. I remember riding across town several times to visit the Trotter family who were friends and former members of our church. He was fun to be around at the church and in school environments. He had the attribute to make everyone feel good about themselves. He showed me that one of the important qualities to have is treating everyone the same.

School Faculty: Role Models and Heroes

Recently I went to the funeral of Coach Frank Singleton. What a great Christian man he was. He had gone to the University South Carolina after World War II. He had boxed and played football while in college. He was my science teacher at Heyward Gibbes Junior High. He also had been one of my B-team coaches at Eau Claire High School. During the funeral service, I thought how Coach Singleton was one of my role models. He had Christian values. Coach was a man's man. He was a stern taskmaster, but at the same time he was fair. His relationship with his students and players was maintained after graduation. He cared about you in school and he cared about you after graduation. In thinking back, I knew Frank for over 62 years. How many people can say they had a relationship with a former teacher for that long. Coach Singleton made a difference in my life.

Here are a couple stories that I remember about Coach Singleton. While in the eighth grade at Heyward Gibbes Junior High School, one of the school toughs picked a fight with me. The fight was because of the nice clothes I was wearing. Although I was not prone to fight, he got my Irish up and once I started swinging, I didn't stop until he was on the ground. As soon as the fight was over, Coach Singleton and BB Rhame, the assistant principal, came running down from the gym admonishing us for fighting. When Coach passed me, he gave me the thumbs-up sign. I learned later that the two had watched the fight from the gym door and didn't intervene until it was over. They both had wanted the tough to learn a valuable lesson.

Another story concerning Coach Singleton involved his former boxing experience. One of the Eau Claire High School football players was playing around and shadow-boxing. Being funny he threw a simulated punch toward Coach. Instinct then took over and without thinking Coach Singleton blocked the punch and threw a punch of his own. The player hit the floor. All that was hurt was the player's feelings. Can you imagine what would have happened in today's environment?

The funeral made me reflect on the teachers I had in junior high school and high school that did more than just teach me, but also helped mold my character and my values. The first person that came to mind was Coach Art Baker. Coach Baker was my Eau Claire High School football and track coach. He was only my track team coach because if his football players didn't play spring sports, they were on the track team. This would keep his football players in shape. He and his family went to College Place Methodist with my family. His Christian values came through in his coaching. I believe Art taught us more about life than football. He taught us that football was a team sport and you could only win if you played as a team. No player is any better than those around him. This translated to life. One lives life as a team player. I have mentioned Coach Baker in other parts of my books. Without question he is one of my heroes and has had a profound impact on my life. Art went on to be head football coach at Furman University, Citadel, and East Carolina University.

A few stories surface that illustrates Coach Baker's firm, but fair leadership. At one of my last football practices my senior year, on the way to the practice field I saw my girlfriend, Jane Miller, nearby. Jane has been my wife for going on 60 years. I proceeded to go see her and receive a hug and a kiss or two. I didn't know that coach was watching. On arriving to practice a few minutes late, he called me over and informed me that I would not start my last game. After starting every game for two years, I would not start my last game. It was obvious that he wanted me to concentrate on football and to be on time. After missing the starting team introductions and not starting on offense, he immediately put me into the game after my replacement was penalized for holding on the first play.

Another story about the coach treating all his players the same way regardless of who they were. It was reported to Coach that our starting quarterback, Thomas Ray, had drunk a glass of champagne after our homecoming game. I don't know how many laps Thomas ran, but it was a lot. Thomas was All-State and played in the Shrine Bowl game. Later he was the starting quarterback for Clemson. His rules were the same for everybody. Our superstars were no exception.

Buddy Robinson, Thomas Ray, and I worked in an icehouse during the summer between our junior and senior year. This was our way of making some money and getting in shape. After work we would go the high school and work out. Workouts back then were mostly running. Since this was summer and practice had not officially started, we were also smoking. Somehow Coach Baker found out, and his discipline for us was imposed soon after he found out. We had been working out, but the intensity then doubled. I can't remember how many sprints we ran, but I can assure you it was substantial. Three starters, two of which were All-State, were punished. Suffice it to say, that we quit smoking. This is the coach that made our football team my senior year arguably the best team in Eau Claire High School's history.

The next person was my line coach. Steve Robertson. He had played football for Newberry College while Coach Baker was the Newberry High School football coach. Steve as a college lineman must have impressed Coach Baker because he brought Steve in to Eau Claire High School to coach his football line how to effectively play. The linemen at Eau Claire immediately related to Coach Robertson. He had done the walk as a college lineman and therefore he earned the right to do the talk. He immediately taught us how important it was for the line to work as a unit. If one player misses his assignment, the designed play fails. Steve's philosophy was if you work hard during practice, you will play well in the games. He made practice very hard and it paid big dividends on game day. The backs on our team were only as good as the linemen in front of them. A high school football team that wasn't accustomed to winning, became a state powerhouse. Coach taught us well. He definitely taught us that success can come with hard work. Coach Baker thought so much of Coach Robertson's ability that he brought him to Furman as one of his coaches. Steve eventually became the assistant head coach at North Carolina State, working under Dick Sheridan, another Eau Claire High School coaching product. Unfortunately for his family, his former players, and the world Steve passed away entirely too soon.

Coach Baker and Coach Robertson were cosponsors of Eau Claire High School's Sportsmen Club. Most of the members in the club were football players. They took us hunting all around the midlands of South Carolina. They cared about us on and off the athletic field. They bonded with us in many ways and led us as Christian leaders. Because of them and Coach Frank Singleton many of us became members of the Fellowship of Christian Athletes (FCA).

Another role model for me was Lily Palmer. She was one of my math teachers. Without question she cared very much for her students. She was very knowledgeable and was able to make complex math concepts easy to understand. When you had a problem understanding a theory or complex math problem, she was always approachable and took the time necessary to make one understand. What she taught, because of the way she taught, was retained. During my first year at South Carolina, because of the math foundation she imparted in me, I sailed through my math courses with ease. The first barrier I hit in math was calculus. How I wished that I had been taught calculus by Ms. Palmer. I know that with her patient instruction, I would have easily grasped these new concepts. I remember hearing from my parents that Ms. Palmer told them in a parent-teacher's conference that with Buster's personality and enthusiasm for life, you don't have to worry about him succeeding. My interpretation would be Buster is not the brightest lightbulb in the room, but he will get the job done. She was a wonderful and caring teacher that made math fun.

Another one of my favorite teachers was Eldene Devet. She taught me English and Speech. Right up front I will tell you that English was not my favorite subject. However, Ms. Devet made the course meaningful. I learned a great deal about sentence structure and correct writing. I learned to enjoy reading. Her teaching style enabled me to absorb and retain knowledge that would be of great help to me in college and in my chosen profession. I might also add that I am very happy with the spellcheck feature on my computer today. Although

I have a natural ability for public speaking or at least I refined the skills over the years, Ms. Devet taught me the basics and the correct techniques. She made me understand how to organize a speech and how to deliver an effective speech. Over the years I have taught many courses and addressed audiences in the hundreds. Ms. Devet taught me well. Her training made a difference in my career and life.

My next influencer was Elizabeth Cardwell. Ms. Cardwell taught me biology and made me love science. Her experiments on dissecting worms and dogfish were exciting and taught me about the world of anatomy. It was exciting for me and I loved her course so much that I majored in biology at the University of South Carolina. Ms. Caldwell was a very knowledgeable teacher that passed her enthusiasm for biology to others. She was also a very patient and understanding teacher. In her later years, Ms. Cardwell was at the Presbyterian Home with my wife's mother, Lavinia Miller. It was a joy for me to tell her how much she had meant to me and that she helped shape my career path. Her eyes became bright and you could feel her sense of satisfaction. She made a difference in my life and I am absolutely sure that I was not the only one.

Eau Claire High School: Once a Shamrock Always a Shamrock

Eau Claire High School was a special institution to many of us. I have mentioned some of the faculty that impacted so many students and remained connected to us for decades after our graduation. The school spirit, at least while I was attending, was off the charts. The whole Eau Claire community was very close then and amazingly the same closeness for many of us has now existed for decades. Even though I have lived all over the country, I have kept in touch with many of my classmates and schoolmates. The spirit of Eau Claire was unique and the times in the 50s, 60s, and 70s were special. It was so special that we don't want to ever let it go. We want to remember the school, the community, the events, and the people forever.

In reflection, what made Eau Claire so special? I believe because it was primarily a community of blue-collar workers. Many of our fathers had fought in World War II and wanted a better world for their families. Parents wanted us to do better than they had. At least while I was going to high school, our sports programs were among the best in central South Carolina. The high school spirit was high and the community supported the teams at home and on the road. We as students liked each other and supported each other. After we graduated, we stayed connected to faculty and to each other.

To illustrate how close many people have remained for decades are the following examples. My class for years had a reunion every five years, until recently. Then the reunions became annual events, at least until the pandemic hit. There is a group of Shamrocks that meet every Wednesday at the Lizard's Thicket in Irmo for breakfast. Attendees at these meetings span over a decade of Eau Claire graduates. There is another group made up of mostly former football players that have a meal together somewhere in the Columbia area on a regular basis. There are many Eau Claire graduates that are in both groups. There are at last three different Facebook groups of former Eau Claire High graduates that are constantly communicating with one another, the numbers increasing daily.

All this being said, Eau Claire was and is special. In talking to friends from other schools, very few have anything close to what I have experienced. Therefore, the term applies, once a Shamrock always a Shamrock. If you say you are a Shamrock to another Shamrock, you have instant creditability.

The University of South Carolina: The Beginning of My Adult Life

Once you graduate from high school, the world as an adult begins. This is an entirely new experience. You learn from your actions and mistakes. The new independence is both exciting and intimidating.

The beginning of my freshman year started with orientation. This was attended by hundreds of my fellow students from around South Carolina, the United States, and the world. I remember that many of high school classmates were attending with me. I am sure that I will not mention everybody, but the ones I am sure that I remember were: Phil Segui, Joe Kinsey, Hank Garrison, Ronnie Barker, Linda Holladay, Marsha Carter, and Gloria Fullbright.

Registering for courses was another of the new processes that was very much a learning experience. Finding courses that fit your schedule and in my case my Sears work schedule was a challenge. Thank goodness, the personnel manager at Sears was most accommodating to the college students that worked for them. Since I was a science major, I had to also factor in afternoon laboratory courses. This further complicated an already very exasperating process. As we got wiser, we had to find out ways to obtain courses that were taught by the most desired and popular professors. Sometimes this led to changing schedules more than one time. Getting the right courses, at the right times, and with the right professor became a science in itself. Our proficiency in accomplishing this mission became more refined in future semesters.

Once classes started, the new challenge was to find the right building and the right classroom in a timely fashion. This caused an immediate understanding for the need to schedule classes in close proximity to each other, especially if they were back-to-back. Since South Carolina had a large campus, course location became a major importance to me. Science courses and general courses like English, math, and history were long ways apart. As freshmen, we had a lot to learn. Oh, the joys of being new on campus.

As classes got started, we became more acclimated and attending class became routine. My first semester went extremely well. My courses were enjoyable and my grades reflected that I learned a great deal. As time went on, I realized, the first semester was a review of what I learned in high school. The second semester was the beginning of a progressively harder curriculum that would take much effort and study outside of the classroom. If you got behind, it became more difficult to catch up. I really found this out with courses like calculus and organic chemistry. College and high school are definitely two different academic worlds. Once you receive your diploma, you have earned it. It was not given to you.

Since most of my high school classmates and schoolmates were day students, during our down time between classes, we would spend time in the student-union at the Russell House. Sometimes we would grab a quick meal, study, and over time some of us started playing bridge. This allowed us to have some fun and meet some of the students living on campus. This became a distraction to some among us and bridge became their main course of study. Unfortunately, some of our peers were no longer allowed to maintain enrollment after their first year. Learning to manage your time wisely and focusing on what is most important is a major outcome of acquiring a college education.

One of my Eau Claire classmates, Hank Garrison, lived in a dormitory on campus. Aa a result, many of the young men from Eau Claire would visit him and his roommate. Laddie Rowell, who was from Lake City, SC. Laddie was paying for his education by growing tobacco on land that his father had allocated to him. For some reason this impressed me. I remember one time Joe Kinsey and I were letting off steam by sparring with each other. On one occasion, I zigged when I should have zagged and Joe popped me in the mouth. I don't know who was more surprised me or Joe. Since I outweighed him by fifty pounds, I believe he was worried about what might be coming. We both laughed and let it go. This is just one example of how we spent time between classes.

After our freshman year, Hank Garrison no longer lived on campus. At times we would go to his house and hang out between classes. He had a pool table and at times we would play a few games. On one occasion we made a small wager. I thought I was a pretty good pool player. I certainly did not factor in that this was his pool table and that he practiced and played pool on a regular basis. It goes without saying he cleaned my plow. We went double or nothing with the same results. This happened several times in row. A small bet had become fairly large. He was a gentleman and let it go. It was years later when I took Hank to a few South Carolina football games that I felt I had paid off the pool wager. He feels the same way.

Several people I knew from Boys State wanted me to rush for a fraternity. This was something that really didn't interest me. Since I had been in the Les Traniers in high school, the fraternity initiation and hazing did not impress me. By that time, I thought it was somewhat of an immature process. This was probably my way of rationalizing it away. The real reason is I couldn't afford it. After November, when my girlfriend, Jane Miller, and I ran away and got married, the expense of being in a fraternity would have wrecked and sunk our financial boat. As it turned out, one of my friends, Bobby DeLoach, was PIKA, a cousin, EY Turner, was in ATO, and a friend, Dub Davis, from Winnsboro, was president of KS. As a result, Jane and I were regularly invited to fraternity parties. Although I was constantly courted by a few fraternities, it was never seriously in the financial tea leaves. I have never been really disappointed that I didn't pledge a fraternity. Years later the U.S. Jaycees would become my fraternity.

As a side story, the *Playboy* magazine every year had a poll and ranked the top ten party schools in the nation. Every year the University South Carolina and University of Miami were always prominent among poll members. My sophomore year, neither school was among the top ten. There was a footnote that stated that South Carolina and Miami were ineligible because they were considered professional party schools.

A fact to back up this claim, in any semester, some fraternities were placed on probation for major school violations. One example of the types of violations that occurred was one fraternity sent party invitations to girls at all female institutions throughout South Carolina. In the invitation was a condom. The last statement in the invitation was, "If you are not interested, please give the invitation to someone who is." Years later our son, Robert, went to Mercer University in Macon, Georgia. Jane and I were relieved because it was a Baptist school. Robert was an extrovert and social animal. Mercer would certainly be a tamer environment for him than other institutions like Georgia and Georgia Tech. We were absolutely wrong. The *Playboy* poll for party schools in 1987 included Mercer University in the top ten.

The other highlights from my college years were attending South Carolina football and basketball games. I remember after one very hot and humid early September football game that I had the best beer ever. Several of us went to a college dive after the game and I ordered a Budweiser in a bottle. It was the coldest and most refreshing beer that I have ever drank. I remember attending basketball games in the old Carolina Fieldhouse. The Carolina Fieldhouse had a seating capacity of about 3000 fans. This compares to the present basketball venue that seats more than 18,000 fans. When sitting on the sidelines, you were close enough to touch the players. I remember at a Duke basketball game where their star, Art Heyman, almost sat in my lap. I enjoyed Carolina sports then and I enjoy them now.

The type of activities mentioned above pretty well ceased after my sophomore year. Jane and I set up housekeeping. At his point, my main activities were with her, classwork, homework, and my job at Sears. During the summer I worked at Sears at night and weekends and during the day drove a truck for the highway department carrying license plates to all 46 counties. Of course, Jane was working full-time at South Carolina Electric and Gas. Now looking back, Jane and I had to mature and become independent quickly. This would greatly help us when we were transferred to Mississippi a few years later. There we had no family and had to manage life on our own. The maturity we gained during my last two years of college would pay big dividends there.

Assassination of a President

While I was in college, while listening to the radio on my way to work at Sears, I heard that President John F. Kennedy had been shot. The report stated that he had been shot as his motorcade was moving through Dallas on the way to a scheduled event. It also stated that Texas Governor John Connolly had also been shot. The driver in the car beside me at a stoplight and I were horrified at the news. I will always remember the date of November 22, 1963. When I got to work, workers and customers were all gathered around televisions to hear updates from Parkview Hospital about the President's condition. There was mutual concern without regard to politics. As more time passed, it was announced that President John F. Kennedy was dead. With the announcement, there was complete silence at Sears and I could see people crying and in prayer. This was without any doubt a national tragedy.

Over the next several days, Jane and I were glued to the television for updates on the shooting. Everyone wanted to know who was responsible and why the president was shot. Was it an individual acting alone or was it a conspiracy? Was it an action by one of our nation's enemies? Was it the Mafia? Many different questions were raised and even after 60 years there are still many theories and scenarios. I have read numerous books and have my own theory on the event as do many other Americans.

I remember the apprehension of Lee Harvey Oswald and seeing him being shot by Jack Ruby as he was led into the Dallas Police Headquarters on national television. Jane was cooking a meal and I was watching the television when it happened. The two of us could not believe what had just happened on a live broadcast. Oswald's assignation created additional speculation and theories. The more that was found out, the more complex the assassination became. One person saw this. A doctor noticed this. Police had many different angles to their investigations and their findings. A Warren Commission headed by U.S. Supreme Chief Justice Earl Warren was established to investigate the assassination. After many months of investigation their findings were sealed for decades because of national security. This certainly added to the confusion to what had happened and why. To this day American people still really do not know all the findings and their implications.

The funeral for our fallen leader was expansive, regal, sad, and thought-provoking all at the same time. Of course, it was all on national television. For all practical purposes the day of the funeral became a holiday for most Americans. Grief was profound for the president's family, close family friends, and the Nation. You could see it and feel it.

I have written about the assassination to highlight how it impacted me and to show how it is still vividly in my memory today. I also remember assassination attempts on Presidents Gerald Ford and Ronald Reagan. Both were horrible and upsetting to me as an American, but the immediate effects and the long-lasting memory of these events do not come close to what I experienced with the Kennedy assassination.

Our First Home: A Small and Quaint Duplex

Jane and I told everyone that we had run away to Abbeville, SC and got married during our freshmen year in college. By the way that was almost a full year after we eloped. We agreed that Jane would finish her sophomore year at Winthrop College. Toward the end of the school year, we decided to set up housekeeping in Columbia. She would give up her education to help me get my degree. This required two things to happen. One was for her to find a job and the other was for us to find a suitable housing. The father, JW Derrick, of Jane's childhood friends, Jean and Joan, got her a good job in customer service at South Carolina Electric and Gas where he worked. Chuck MacInnis, our brother-in-law, had a friend, Corky Gains, who was getting ready to move out of a duplex that he was renting. We quickly located the duplex owner and placed a deposit. The quaint duplex at 1523 Gladden Street was ours. It was is in nice area about three blocks off of Millwood Avenue. The apartment was an upstairs unit with stairs that led to the front door which faced the street.

Once Corky moved out, we took possession. It was obvious from examining the apartment that it would require some touchup. The touchup became repainting the whole apartment including the baseboards. My parents, Paul and Polly Turner, a family handyman, OT Barr, Jane, and I spent a long weekend finishing the task. Boy did it look great when we finished. Now we had to furnish the apartment. Thanks to my parents and Jane's mother, Lavinia Miller, they donated some furniture to us and bought a few pieces that added to the assortment. Family friends, Woody and Helen Weed and Joe and Norma Castles, gave us some furniture and loaned us other pieces. By the time everything was in place, I thought our first home was magnificent. We went from nothing to a furnished apartment in a couple of weeks.

Looking back, we are very appreciative to my parents and Jane's mother for what they did for us and how they helped us develop a strong foundation for our journey together. We will always be indebted to Jane's sister, Ethel, and her husband, Chuck. They were our friends and supported us in so many ways the entire time that we lived in the duplex. They all gave us an example about how important family is and what a difference it made in our lives. Of course, grandparents and family friends contributed to our spiritual wellbeing.

In a very short time, we used our apartment to entertain family and friends. My cousins, Roy and Johnny Neville, would bring their dates, Charlotte Orr and Barbara Lane, to our apartment on weekends. Both couples eventually married. The standard fare was hamburgers and homemade French fries. Then we would play canasta. We kept a running total score that eventually was over a million. Inexpensive fun that is still high on our list of things that we enjoyed most. I might add that Roy, Charlotte, and Barbara still remember these good times. Other classmates and friends joined us for fun get-togethers. I remember Phil Segui, Harriet Varn, Robert Golf, Dondra Dell, Jenky Farmer, Bob Simon, Lollie Barton Cowart and the list goes on and on. You can add to the list of people that were routinely at the apartment our parents and grandparents. This was especially true after our son, Paul III, was born. Once you have a social calendar and love, an apartment becomes a home.

My senior year at South Carolina Jane became pregnant or we became pregnant. We were excited and anxious at the same time. I still believe the course, comparative anatomy, that I took in summer school caused her to become pregnant. We made a decision to save more money and to pay the car payment and apartment rental ahead a few months. This way we could manage everything else with the money that I made at my part-time job at Sears and Roebuck. Once Paul III was born, we had to worry about daycare. Another of God's great miracles happened. I was alerted that Charlie White, a Carolina football player, who I knew was graduating and needed to find work for the lady who was keeping his child. Their lady, Betty Haigler, became Paul III's nanny. What special care she gave to our son. She loved him so much that she wanted to go with us when we were transferred by the Centers for Disease Control (CDC) to Mississippi. Can you imagine the three of us and Betty in a very small three-bedroom house together? We cared so much for Betty that we found her a job before we left Columbia.

A couple other vivid memories that are still with me after all these years are as follows. About the time Paul III was born, we knew we would need a washing machine. JW Derrick's sister, Flo, worked at Cate McLaurin Appliances and was able to get us a washing machine at a good price. My daddy and I went and got it. Once we were at the duplex, it was necessary for us to haul it on a dolly up a steep and narrow set of metal steps in the back of the duplex. The steps looked like the fire escapes that you see on high-rise buildings on television. Daddy and I manhandled the washing machine and dolly up the stairs. Half- way up we got stuck. It took an effort and maneuvering to get it untangled. At this point daddy was struggling and I was scared he was having a health issue. Thanks goodness, we were able to finish our task. Although daddy was exhausted, with some rest, he bounced back and was fine. As a side story, these steel stairs were a nightmare when they got icy or wet. After a few close calls, Jane and I started to enter the apartment from the front door during inclement weather.

The other memory was that after entertaining some guest one night, on looking out the window, I saw a man peeping into the girls' apartment next door. I called them and asked if there was any reason that a man would be in the bushes and looking into their window. When they said no, I told them to call the police. I retrieved my trusty double-barrel shot gun, sneaked down the back steps, and then literally scared him out of the bushes and down the street. The police arrived and wrote up a report. They suspected that since the young women worked at a nearby bank, some customer had become enamored with one of them. From that point on, all three complexes became more vigilant. By the way, all the tenants were females, but me. On another occasion, at the duplex on the other side, female undergarments were taken during the day while they were working. After this occasion, I went and bought Jane a .38 caliber pistol to have while I was working late. I also taught her how to use it safely. She still has this pistol in the glove compartment of her car today.

We enjoyed the duplex and the neighborhood for four years, until we were transferred to Mississippi. We still have very good memories of our first home.

What a Send-Off

While we were at the University of South Carolina together, Buddy Robinson married Lynn Madden. I don't remember everyone in the wedding party, but I do remember that Phil Segui and I were groomsmen. We, along with the other groomsmen, had the responsibility to send Buddy and Lynn off on their honeymoon in a significant way.

Once we located the car to be used for the honeymoon, we did the usual decorating and tied cans on strings from the rear bumper. It is probably worth mentioning that the paint we used would not injure the vehicle in any way. The rest of the sendoff is another story. Someone, and I know it wasn't Phil or me, rigged some type of device to the ignition. I know that I didn't do it, because I am not mechanical enough to have done it. It would explode when the car was started. Another person in our party put some type of raw fish, I think it was mackerel, in the heater of the car. Since it was cold, the idea was the smelly fish would permeate the car when the heater was cut on.

After the wedding ceremony and the reception, Buddy and Lynn were ready to depart. Lynn threw her bouquet over her head to be caught by one of her attendants. Then to the car they raced. To our collective disappointment the expected bang did not occur. However, in the next block a loud bang was heard and smoke bellowed from under the hood of the car. It obviously was an annoyance, but it must have not done any damage, because Buddy never slowed down. Phil, the rest of the wedding party, and I rolled in laughter. I never had the courage to ask Buddy about whether they ever smelled the mackerel. The joys of being young and making fun of everything, including the sacred bond of marriage.

Have Another Falstaff, Partner

At some time about my senior year at the University of South Carolina, Jane and I with a bunch of our friends went to Myrtle Beach. I don't remember everyone in our party, but I do remember Phil Segui. Phil and I both enjoyed watching the *Baseball Game of the Week* with Dizzy Dean and Pee Wee Reese. Both announcers were legendary Baseball Hall of Fame players. Dizzy was a pitcher and Pee Wee was a shortstop. Their delivery of the play-by-play made each game interesting and lively. Dizzy was as much an entertainer as an announcer. His home-spun stories kept you chuckling throughout the game. The game was sponsored by Falstaff Beer. One of us wondered how many times during each game that the pair would say, have a Falstaff, partner. We didn't know, but we decided to find out during the upcoming Saturday game. We also decided to have some fun in answering the question by buying a case of Falstaff. We pledged to drink a Falstaff beer each time one of the announcers would say have a Falstaff, partner. Prior to the game, we bought the case of beer and iced it down in a large cooler. Right off the bat, Dizzy said, "Have a Falstaff beer, partner." We were off and running. I can't tell you how many beers we both drunk, but by the end of the game the tub was almost empty. We couldn't tell you how many times Dizzy and Pee Wee promoted the beer, but it had to be a lot. Between drinking beer and relieving ourselves, Phil and I lost count. At the end of the game, we were feeling no pain. It goes without saying, Jane and Phil's date were not very happy with us. To this day, I can still see Dizzy, saying, "Have a Falstaff, partner."

A Memorable Field Botany Trip

In less than a month after our first son, Paul III, was born, my botany class went on a field trip to Mount Le Conte in the Great Smoky Mountains National Park. The field trip would be led by my favorite professor, Dr. Wade Batson. He was very knowledgeable and was without question the most personable professor I had ever had during my studies at the

University of South Carolina. He treated all his students as if they had value and made us feel like family. He had already had our class to his home to meet his family and to enjoy a meal. The main purpose of the trip was to learn about the different vegetation indigenous to the Great Smoky Mountain's National Park with special emphasis on those trees and plants at the higher elevations. We would find different species and key out the plants using the techniques that Dr. Batson had taught us. Of course, we would use our trusty guides to help identify each plant correctly. With our professor as our guide, we took a University bus to the base of Mount Le Conte.

Now the adventure was to begin. Our first mission was to climb to the top of the mountain which by the way is one of the tallest mountains east of the Mississippi River. The trail is narrow and on some stretches of the trail one must be very careful and pay close attention to avoid a potentially dangerous fall. We all headed up the mountain at our own pace and with a few people in each party. Our goal was to reach the cabins at the top before dark. The cabins would be our lodging and the place for our meals while we were there.

As we arrived at the cabins, we were impressed at the serenity which they projected against the evening sky. We were all amazed to found out that most of the building materials for the cabins had been brought up the mountain by mules and donkeys. Some building supplies had been actually brought up the mountain on the backs of climbers. Food stocks are still brought up on the backs of mules. We were all assigned to different cabins for our lodging. At the appointed time we all met for supper in the dining lodge. I guess the rigors of the climb and the mountain air gave the whole party a hearty appetite. The food was amazingly good and everyone consumed more food than usual, at least I know I did. After the meal, Professor Batson gave us an introduction on what we could expect the next day. After the lecture, we headed to our respective cabins. My cabin patrons with little fanfare went to bed and asleep quickly.

The next morning, I rose early as usual and went outside to look at the fabulous view of the majestic Great Smoky Mountains from the top of Mount Le Conte. The view was breathtaking and any words to describe what I saw would not do it justice. It was a good morning to be alive. As I stood their admiring the scenic beauty, I smelled the alluring scent of bacon cooking. I was sure that breakfast would be as good or better than dinner.

After breakfast Dr. Batson gave us our last instructions and we headed off in teams to collect our specimens of various mountain plant life to be keyed and identified. The diverse and different trees and plants were abundant and the specimens we collected became significant in a short period. Once back at the camp, we stayed busy identifying what we had found. The Great Smoky Mountains National Park has a vigorous botany that is entirely different from what you find in central South Carolina. The trip, the camp, and our discoveries made memories that have lasted for a lifetime. The fact that I am writing this story 55 years later attest to these wonderful memories.

One last memory happened on my hike down Mount Le Conte. The trail we used to return to our bus was different from the trail we had used to climb to the top. At any rate, I was pretty well hiking by my-self. I heard a noise from behind me. I assumed it was others in our group catching up with me. Looking over my shoulder, I could not see anyone. The noise got louder. This time when I looked, I was not happy with what I saw. A large black bear was coming down the trail behind me and was getting closer. I was in a predicament and won-dered what should I do. Time for a lot of thinking about the problem was diminishing by the second. My decision was that the bear could have the trail all to himself. Without fanfare, I climbed, fell, or a little of both down the mountain. The bear never slowed down and went right past me to my delight. After I got my composure, I climbed back up to the trail and headed for the bus. Without overstating my concern, for the rest of my hike I was cautious about my surroundings and was very conscious of every strange sound.

A great trip and great memories went with me back to Columbia to see my wife, Jane, and our young son, Paul III.

Art Work Appreciated Then and Now

Sometime right before Paul III was born and I graduated, Jane and I visited an art show at Columbia Mall. There was art work by a number of amateur artists. It was amazing and exciting to see the different styles. We were impressed by how good many if these individuals were. At one booth, we fell in love with a rural scene outside the small town of Irmo. Since Jane and I loved the outdoors, we really identified with the fall scene that featured an old homestead with an outhouse during the fall or winter. It was well done. We asked the artist, W.H. Yeamans, how much he wanted for the painting. He told us the price. It was more than we could afford on our limited budget. Mr. Yeamans asked us what we could afford and then told us, if it didn't sell, he would accept what we could pay. Toward the end of the show, we went back to his booth. He had the framed art work already wrapped and waiting for us. Jane and I suspected that he saw how much a young couple really liked his art work and wanted us to have it. We later learned that W.H. Yeamans was a chemical engineer that worked for Allied Chemical in Irmo.

This was the first original art work that we procured. We liked it very much then and we love it now. We proudly hang the scene over the fireplace in our great room.

"Carolina Forever to Thee"

The Turner family has always been faithful to the University of South Carolina (USC). My Uncle Gene, Walter Eugene Turner, was the first in my grandfather, Paul Crawford Turner's, family to graduate from USC. I was the second to graduate. Now we have many in our family who have attended and graduated from this great institution which opened its doors in 1801. Suffice it to say we supported USC academically, but Carolina sports was our passion. Uncle Gene and his wife, Devon, my cousin, Roy Neville, and I were probably the most zealous supporters. Gene and Devon followed the Gamecocks and attended a plethora of athletic events. Sometimes attending several events in a week. My earliest memories were going to football games with my daddy as a child. Later, I would attend games with my high school football coaches and other players. While in college I attended both basketball and football games. After Jane and I set up housekeeping, she and I both would attend games. After graduation and being transferred a couple years later, I keep up with South Carolina athletics by radio, television, and newspapers. In Mississippi and Texas, Jane and I would attend in person if a game was nearby. I remember attending football games with Georgia, Old Miss, and Mississippi State while we lived in Jackson. We attended a Baylor game while we lived in Austin. This is a long way of saying that the Turner family and my immediate family loved USC sports and supported them whether they won or loss.

A side story, Big Jim Poston and his date accompanied Jane and me to see the Baylor football game. Jim and I had become friends in the Austin Jaycees. Jim had been one of South Carolina's most outstanding defensive linemen in the late 1960s and played several years of professional football. At 6 feet six inches tall and weighing more than 300 pounds, he was a man's man. I had no reservations whatsoever when we went into a bikers' bar together. I felt totally safe. Years later, when Jane and I had moved to Haywood County, I looked forward to reconnecting with Jim. I had been told he had moved back home from Texas. To my dismay, I found that he had indeed moved back home, but had succumbed to a major heart attack at 45 years of age.

When I was transferred to Atlanta, I took my enthusiasm to a higher level. I joined the Gamecock Club, USC booster club, and as I write, I have been a member for 44 years. At one point, I was president of the Atlanta Gamecock Club for five years. As a result, I was a member of the University of South Carolina Gamecock Club Board of Directors in Columbia. We met regularly and conducted club business and developed ways to financially support the athletic program and at the same time develop policy and benefits for our membership. As a board member, I was instrumental in pushing through policy changes that benefited the average Gamecock Club member. All benefits were slanted toward the large donors which were mostly companies. They got the best tickets for home games, away games, and bowl games. My motions leveled the playing field. Instead of getting several of the best tickets at a time, they were limited to two until the lower giving levels had an opportunity to obtain prime tickets. Since most corporations give their tickets away, this allowed the real Gamecock booster to receive better tickets. The second motion that I made was to give priority points for each year that you were a member of the Gamecock Club. This rewarded loyalty. When seasons were going to be good, the fat cats would swoop in and take the best seats. When seasons were going to be lean, they would disappear. I don't think I made my old coach, Art Baker, very happy. His job as Associate Athletic Director and the Director of the Gamecock Club was raising funds for athletics. I had reduced the effectiveness of a couple of his fund-raising tools. My job was to look out for the membership.

Tailgating and football games go hand in hand. Both enhance the other. My daddy, Paul, and mother, Polly, tailgated for years with three other couples: the Hipps, the Weeds, and the Derricks. All four men had worked for years together at Claussen's Bakery. Slick Derrick would drive out early on game day to the Farmers' Market which was right across the street from the football stadium and reserve a prime tailgating spot. Over the years he started getting the same spot for every game. I believe he gave some money to the vendor to make this possible. Hours before the game they would gather, drink, and eat until about an hour before game time. Then they would cross the street to the game. Jane and I started joining them for these wonderful events. The food and adult beverages were unbelievable. The camaraderie and fellowship were even better. Other family members and friends that they knew would come over to say hello and partake in some of the merriment. Our sons, Paul III and Robert, joined us for many of these games.

One of the memories that I treasure from this time period was when I invited Bill and Marge Watson to attend a game. Bill attended South Carolina and was the Deputy Director of the Centers for Disease Control (CDC). Jane couldn't come. I was hurrying from Stone Mountain to Columbia to meet Bill and Marge at Daddy and Mother's home. I was in a hurry because I didn't want to be late. As I drove, I became sleepy. I felt that I didn't have time to rest. Sometime later, I woke up from falling asleep in the middle of the median on Interstate 20. A bridge-abutment was about 20 feet in front of the car. I had come close to being in a bad accident. At the next exit, I pulled over and rested. From that day forward, when I felt sleepy while driving, I would pull off at the next exit and rest (sleep). When I got to my parents' home, Bill and Marge were already there. They were enjoying each other. You would have thought they had been raised together. Bill and Marge fit right into the tailgating get-together. The fact that Bill, Mike Hipp, Woody Weed, and Slick Derrick were all World War II veterans, increased the bonding. South Carolina upset the mighty Southern California Trojans that day. This added to the occasion. I remember the sticker that was being handed out after the game, "No Trojan can hold our Cocks." Everyone enjoyed the day.

Several years later the tailgating group of my parent's friends ceased to exist. Age and health problems took a toll. In place of the old group of tailgaters came a new group of tailgaters. Daddy and I served as the nucleus. It initially included Jane, our boys, Paul III and Robert, and Jack Weant, one of my daddy's and my friends. Over time, it included Paul III's and Robert's families. As time passed, it included my grandchildren, Andrew, Amanda, Stephanie, and Kelly. After more years passed, our tent (canopy), included my grandchildren's dates and mates. At other times, our tailgating included my friends, Jack's family, Paul III's friends, and Kathy's, Paul III's wife, friends. On some games, we would have a large number in our area. I remember some of my classmates that were included: Henry Hixson, Charles O'Brien, and Hank Garrison. I could go and on and mention many more participates. Some of my more memorial events are described below.

Every year I would buy four season tickets. After several years, two of the tickets that I bought were for Daddy and Jack Weant. The two tickets that I used were under the overhang on the Farmers' Market side of the stadium and up high. I could see the whole field. I loved those seats. My tickets were on the 45-yard line. I kept these tickets for close to forty years. Every year, I worked hard to improve Daddy's and Jack's tickets. I had them on the lower level near the end zone. One day the Gamecock Club office called and told me that my daddy was there and wanted to change his tickets. It seems a young couple and their children were annoying him and Jack during every game. They were rowdy and obstructing their view. Since his tickets were purchased by me and purchased on my Gamecock Club membership, I had to give permission for any change. My instructions to them were to let Daddy go anywhere he wanted to go as long as my two seats on the 45-yard line remained the same. There is another story concerning Daddy and Jack's tickets. At a game that I did not attend, there was a gully-washer. The two of them got totally drenched. The water flowing down the steps by them was higher than the tops of their shoes. Mother said that when Daddy got home, everything he wore to the game was dripping wet. Everything in his bill folder was dripping wet including his folding money.

Because we have several members in the family that have birthdays in September and early October, we picked one football game that we called the birthday weekend. Family birthdays in order were:

Andrew, Kathy, Robert, me, and Stephanie. With Amanda's marriage, we added Joe Norton. I would secure additional tickets for the whole family. This included mates and dates. On this occasion, we sometimes had a dozen or more tailgating. Paul III, Kathy, Jane, and I would bring an assortment of great foods and beverages. Paul III and Kathy would often set up the family and Jack to a meal and beverages after the game at a sports' bar. When we as a family decided it was no longer convenient to attend games and tailgate in Columbia, we have had the birthday weekend get-together at Paul III and Kathy's home. They usually have the event catered. Of course, we now watch several football games, including Carolina games, on television. We still look forward to the family birthday weekend and Paul III and Kathy's saltwater pool adds to the frivolity.

At one game, it was only Paul III, and Kathy, Jack, and me attending. Kathy was preparing some food and was in the process of cutting some summer sausage. She was using one of her husband's razor-sharp skinning knives. The knife slipped and she cut her hand very badly. One of the South Carolina Highway Patrolmen, Shelton, at the front of the Farmers' Market was contacted. Kathy had gone to high school with Shelton. He performed first aid and recommended that she go to the emergency room for stiches. The four of us proceeded to the hospital. While she was being stitched-up, we watched the South Carolina/Florida game in the waiting room. Once she had been released, we, with mutual consent, went to the Ale House and finished watching the game. We ate and drank together and had our usual good time. Kathy had remorse that she had made us miss seeing the game in person. Our mutual sentiment was that Kathy was more important than any football game.

On another football weekend, Jack Weant and I were the only two to attend the game. On the way to the stadium, we stopped at Maurice Bessinger's Piggy Park Barbeque and got our meal. We did our usual tailgating outside Williams Brice Stadium. About an hour prior to the game, we took our long walk to our seats. The game started and we were enjoying the activities on the field. All of sudden Jack started feeling ill. He was clammy and didn't feel very good. In a little while he was getting worse. To his chagrin, I went to the first aid station and got help. Two staff members with a stretcher followed me to our section and took him for evaluation. For a few minutes we were the main event in our section of the stadium. As they took a thorough history, they provided Jack various support such as liquids, oxygen, and various supplements. As Jack responded to the treatment, he began to feel much better. Jack remembered that he may have accidently doubled up on one of his medications. This was the culprit that caused his problem. Over his objections, I decided to take him home. His health was far more important that the game. Since he had driven us to the game in his car, I drove us back to his home. I called Jane who was visiting her sister, Ethel, and had her meet me at Jack's house in Lexington. All ended well and both Jack and I were relieved.

In actuality, football and tailgating were the nucleus for bringing family and friends together. The football game was no more important than the tailgating. Together that made socializing the main reward. Win or lose, the Turner family supports the Gamecocks.

The Smallest Bladder Award

I still remember a trip that my cousin, Roy Neville, his wife, Charlotte, Buzzy and Jo Holland, Daddy, and I made to a Clemson versus South Carolina football game. Because of Daddy's insistence, we stopped at every rest stop between Columbia and Clemson. That is going and returning from the game. In addition, restrooms were used every time we stopped for gas or food. I never knew why the frequent stops were required. It could have been a bladder infection or that daddy just had a small bladder. At any rate, we all lost count of the number of restroom breaks.

Once we arrived on the Clemson campus, we parked and set up

for our tailgate experience which included food and adult beverages. Then the adventure really started. Shortly after having a beer, Daddy informed me that he had to go to the restroom. You need to understand back then that parking and tailgating was done all over the Clemson campus. There were no such things as portable toilets. Daddy and I went off in search of a facility. After some time and some distance, we found what we needed. After relieving ourselves, we returned to our parking area. After another beer, we started the same trip once again. This was repeated at least one more time. We went to the necessary prior to finding our seats, during the game, and after the game. It made me conclude that my daddy had one of the smallest bladders known to man. Roy, Buzzy, and I still laugh when we remember this trip.

Buzzy, a retired dentist in Columbia, and I recently were talking and on remembering this occasion, chuckled once again. Buzzy divulged that he had a bladder infection at the same time and this was requiring the need for rest stops. Therefore, he was happy that the frequent stops were occurring. It is always amazing to me how little things like this trip create lasting wonderful memories. My dad was special and loved by many.

All for One, One for All

In the fall, after I went to work in the South Carolina Venereal Disease Program, one day I was the only one in the clinic. I was called to the front desk where I found a young man who needed some help for a very private matter. On taking him back to my cubicle, I found out that he had a drip from his private anatomy. On examination in the clinic area, it appeared to me that he had gonorrhea. The doctor confirmed my suspicion. The young man was given a dose of penicillin. While he was waiting the required time to see if he tolerated the medication, I interviewed him. He had become attracted to a waitress at the Wade Hampton Hotel. Very quickly after their meeting, they had sex. Since she was the only one with whom he had relations, it was obvious she was the source of his infection. In those days we really only investigated syphilis cases, the young man was sent on his way with instructions not to have sexual relations for several days.

A few days later, I was asked for specifically by name by another young man and on examination, he also had gonorrhea. I went through the same process and found out this young man had had sex with the same Wade Hampton Hotel waitress. It my interview, I found out that this young man was a fraternity brother of my first case. For the next several days, fraternity brother after fraternity brother came to the Richland County Health Department asking to see Mr. Turner. Since they knew that I graduated from the University of South Carolina and what they said to me was confidential, I received the trust of this fraternity. Soon I had the trust of other campus fraternities. The head clerk told me that I had become the best-known venereal disease investigator that they had ever had and in a very short time at that.

Although, as I previously stated, we didn't normally investigate gonorrhea cases, in this instance, my boss felt that we needed to find this young lady and treat her before she infected every fraternity at USC. I found her and brought her to be treated. She made a pass at me on the way to the clinic. On interviewing this lady, she without question liked sex. The number of sexual encounters she had in a week was staggering. She was clearly a nymphomaniac. Being pretty and ready, she had quickly enticed a whole fraternity. The fraternity motto "All for one, and one for all" had cost this group dearly.

A Special Mentor and Friend

I was hired by the National Communicable Disease Center (CDC) right out of college. My first assignment was to the South Carolina Venereal Disease Control Program. I was assigned counties in central South Carolina with my headquarters being the Richland County Health Department in Columbia. In my first book, "Tells of a Southern Boy: A Life in Stories," I told many stories about my memories and experiences while working in South Carolina. The county manager for the Richland County Venereal Program was George Dewey Bennett. George was a career U.S. Army veteran that had fought in both World War II and in Korea. He had gone from being an enlisted man to an officer, a major, receiving battlefield commissions. After the Korean War, the size of the Armed Forces was reduced and he was reduced in rank to a Command Chief Master Sergeant. He ran the local VD program like a Command Chief Master Sergeant. George was a big man and at times he would have strong disagreements with both State and Federal VD management. The Richland County Health Director, Dr. John Preston, almost always supported George's position. Although I had a federal supervisor, for the most part when I was in Richland County, I worked for George. I don't know of any reason why, but George and I became friends. I believe it could have been because he had no children and I was about the same age of a son if he had had one.

His wife, Olive, and George routinely invited Jane and me to their house for many get-togethers and meals. Jane and I felt comfortable being with them in their beautiful house that was near the entrance to Fort Jackson. George appeared to know everyone in Columbia and at Fort Jackson. He and I routinely ate at Henry's Restaurant and we were always treated like royalty. Later, I found out that he was part owner. He took me under his wing and taught me all that he knew. He became like a special uncle. His associates became my associates. This was particularly true when I had business at Fort Jackson. When I had venereal disease business at the pre-induction center and the dermatology clinic, officers and non-commission officers treated me with courtesy and respect. This was mainly because of George's influence.

Over time, I learned a few stories that were related to his time in the army. He was medic during the Korean War and became a prisoner of war. He told me about how helpless he felt when he couldn't obtain medicines, like penicillin, to help his fellow imprisoned GIs. He had many to die before his very eyes. When he told me this story, he had tears in his eyes. Another story he told me took place in World War II. It concerned a high-ranking Shah in the Middle East. The Shah's son was badly sick and close to death. George was asked to help him. George treated the son with what I believe was penicillin. The son fully recovered. In gratitude for George's success, the Shah presented George a jewel-encrusted knife. He showed me the knife and let me handle it. The gems were radiant and without question were very valuable. Eventually, George told me that the fabulous piece would be mine upon his death. Suffice it to say that upon his death, I never received it. However, the thought to me was what was important.

Before I left South Carolina, I became a Master Mason. At my induction ceremony were fellow Masons: my Daddy, my two grandfathers, George, and my assistant CDC state representative, Ed Shearin. George was like family. I might add that Ed was too. Ed and I have communicated regularly over the years.

Once I was transferred, for years when we came home to Columbia, Jane and I would visit George and Olive. They were special people and friends. Unfortunately, all of us will pass from this world and George and Olive passed to the Father's kingdom. He will always be remembered for how good he was to me and how much he taught me. Rest in peace, my friend, you deserve it.

Five Generations of Family: A Special Event

In the first year of my oldest son, Paul III's, life, Jane and I took him to meet his great-great- grandmother, Nellie Angel Hampton. My grandparents, Robert and Cartie Boykin, and my parents, Paul and Polly Turner, accompanied us on the trip. This was indeed a special occasion. Paul III represented the fifth living generation in the Hampton family. It was so special and unique that the *Asheville Citizen Times* came and took a picture and featured a story about the event in the paper. The five generations were Big Mimi, my Mimi, my mother, me, and Paul III. Big Mimi went on to have many other great-great-grand-children. Since people don't get married as early as they did in the past, the chances of having five living generations in a family is now very rare. I would like to be both healthy and mentally sound and be able to see my great-great-grandchildren. It is possible, but not likely.

Another story concerning our visit to see Big Mimi. It was a special occasion and many family members came to experience the event and, of course, to visit the South Carolina part of the clan. Late on the afternoon while visiting with her, we asked innocently, if we could do anything for her. She simply said, "Son, I would like a good drink of whiskey." Therefore, without discussion my daddy and I went to a nearby liquor store and bought a bottle of a good bourbon. On our return, Big Mimi had herself a sizable drink. Some family members didn't really appreciate the occasion. My daddy and I reasoned, if the matriarch of a very large family that still has her mental faculties wanted a drink, she should get a drink. I hope when I am old and have a special request that if it is not totally unreasonable, that some-one in my family will supply it.

The Engine That Would Not Die

In 1970, Jane and I bought a relatively new 1968 Plymouth Valiant from my Mimi Boykin. She decided that she wasn't going to drive anymore and we needed a second car. With all the traveling that I was doing, Jane really needed a car to use while I was gone. The Valiant was a practical car that gave very good gas mileage. The en-gine was a slant-six that was half of an airplane engine. It proved to be very durable and performed well. This vehicle was with the Turner family for 17 years. The car was from an age that if a car could give you 100,000 road-miles, you felt blessed. When this car was sold to a salvage yard after a wreck my son, Robert, had, the speedometer exceeded 187,000 miles. The car was salvaged because we couldn't find another front end for a 1968 Plymouth Valiant. Salvage yards all over metropolitan Atlanta were contacted with no success. There is no doubt that the engine would still have been good for many more miles. Wouldn't you know it, several months after we salvaged the Valiant, I passed a similar year Plymouth Valiant near our deer camp in Monticello, Georgia. For a couple of hundred dollars, I could have bought the whole car and I would have had a good front end that I needed. With repair and good paint job, she would have been good for several more years. The she is because I called my car with affection "Maudine." It would have been interesting to know how many more miles were left on the marvelous engine. There are a few stories related to this car.

Jane used the car for years shuttling the boys around. Once we had bought Jane a new car, I used this car as my work vehicle in Mississippi, Texas, and Georgia. I took very long trips to our regional offices while I was in Texas. Sometimes I put over 1000 miles on the car in one week. It was like a Timex watch, "It took a licking and kept on ticking." When the original paint on the car started to fade, I had it repainted. Once being renewed, it continued to look sharp and performed well. In seventeen years, other than routine maintenance, the repairs were minimal. Great car and certainly a great return on our investment of $1500.

The only problem I ever had on the open highway while driving the Valiant was in Texas. It was right after I had bought some new Firestone 721 tires. The grooves on the lug nuts and bolts for the car were reversed, I guess to improve safety. The technician in mounting the new tires didn't realize that was the case and sheared off several lug bolts. He obviously was afraid he was going to be disciplined and have to pay for the damage out of his own pocket. Therefore, he told nobody about his mistake. On a trip from Austin to Houston, the tires on the Plymouth started to react like they were badly out of balance. On examination, I found one tire was held on by only two lugs. That is three bolts out of five were gone. I found lugs and bolts missing on other tires. This was very dangerous. I called and had a wrecker tow my car to the nearest Firestone dealership. After having several lug bolts replaced, I completed my trip. I had come close to having a major problem and potentially a major wreck with injury. When I got back to Austin, I returned to the Firestone store where I had bought the tires and gave the manager a piece of my mind. I emphasized how much of a hazard this had been. The dealership compensated me for my inconvenience and this was mild when you think what their lability would have been had their negligence resulted in a wreck and injury.

Both my sons, Paul III and Robert, both learned to drive in the Valiant. They had no problem driving the Valiant, but neither one liked dating in this durable and efficient car. Its stark lines and antique style would not get the job done. They always wanted to use their mother's car which was always the newer car in the family and much classier. Jane's Buick LeSabre was always the preferred car.

A Menu That Was in French

Right after I was transferred from South Carolina to Mississippi, the Centers for Disease Control (CDC) sent me to learn how to conduct a mass immunization program. The first afternoon was spent learning how to break down and clean a hypospray-jet-injector which was used to administer vaccines. This electric instrument or the foot-operated version would be used to immunize millions of people worldwide. Don Stenhouse from CDC headquarters in Atlanta was the instructor. Don and I were destined to become friends and work closely together several years later in the Division of Immunizations. Once the training was over, the rest of the afternoon was free time. The New Orleans immunization campaign that I was supposed to observe was the next day. After happy hour at a Bourbon Street bar, several of us headed to a famous New Orleans restaurant, Antoine's, in the French Quarter. I don't remember who selected it, but I do know it wasn't me. A very regal host seated us and provided the group menus. As I scanned the menu, I noticed two things immediately. The first was that the menu was in French. The second was the prices were off the chart. Nothing was even close to the Federal per diem. To add insult to injury, you paid for each course of the meal. Here I am a brand-new GS-9 (Federal pay grade) with a wife and new son. We were going to have to pinch each penny to financially survive. Another problem that I faced was to avoid being embarrassed or thought to be a cheapskate. Therefore, I now had three problems to overcome. French would really not be a problem because price would drive my ordering decisions. Someone in the group suggested ordering wine. My quick response, was, "I really don't want any wine." The price for a bottle of wine was far more than I could afford. Someone asked if I wanted to share crepes. You bet I would. That would mean I would only owe half. The cheapest main course was poulette. I figured that was chicken and that dish would be adequate for me. In spite of my diligence in ordering food items after tip my bill was twice my daily per diem allowance. The restaurant was very elegant and the food although overpriced was very good. It was great experience. Today such an experience would amount to pocket change. At the end of the day, I had eaten well and hadn't been embarrassed.

A New Training for Public Health Advisors

In the second year I was assigned by the Centers for Disease Control (CDC) to Mississippi. Jack Benson, my supervisor in the Atlanta Regional Office, called me and let me know I was one of 20 public health advisors (PHAs) chosen to attend the Epidemic Intelligence Service (EIS) course in July. This was a truly unique opportunity. The EIS course was intended primarily for physicians and veterinarians. This would be the first time that public health advisors were allowed to participate in this prestigious course. On arrival to CDC headquarters, I found out that all 20 of the PHAs attending the course were from state and city immunization programs. We were all younger PHAs and it was felt that CDC could benefit from us attending the course. I learned over time that Dr. David Sencer, CDC Director, and

Bill Watson, Deputy Director of CDC, were great proponents of us attending. Dr. Alex Langmuir, Founder and Chief of the EIS Program, was not an advocate.

This EIS course was two weeks of intense training about epidemiology and statistics. The course included a great deal of laboratory work that included solving outbreak problems using the tools that we were being taught. It became apparent that our medical and veterinarian colleagues were far ahead of us on statistical training. My laboratory partner could have taught the course as well as our actual statistical instructor, Dr. Reid, from Harvard. My partner read *Playboy* magazines during lectures on statistics. On the other hand, the public health advisor group was far ahead of them when it came to shoe leather epidemiology. We had all been trained in the venereal disease program and were very familiar with contact tracing and tracking down cases. We were familiar with collecting outbreak data and using the data to control the outbreaks. In other words, we each had our strengths and weaknesses. We could certainly learn from one another. The laboratory scenarios about a particular outbreak certainly proved this point. An instructor would lay out a disease outbreak problem and then we in teams would have to solve it. The first several laboratory problems were quickly solved by public health advisors. The docs would hypothesize about the disease that we were dealing with. They would come up with a plethora of exotic diseases. Since the PHA's religiously read the CDC Morbidity and Mortality Weekly Report (MMWR), one of us would remember the outbreak that we were being asked to solve. After this happened several times, Dr. Langmuir asked the PHA's to keep the answers to ourselves and let the docs learn. Where we as a group did and then concentrated on learning statistics.

The EIS course training was a great help to me during my career. I investigated a number of disease outbreaks that could have been prevented through immunizations. In Conroe, Texas I found a large number of babies that had received measles vaccine at 9 months of age that were still becoming infected with measles. Running a chi-square, I found this to be strongly significant and alerted headquarters about my findings. A thorough study proved that babies were not converting after being immunized at nine months of age because of maternal antibodies interfering. Eventually, babies were not immunized until one year of age and later that was changed to 15 months of age.

I just recently found out that we were probably the first and last public health advisors to attend the Epidemic Intelligence Service course. Therefore, I am one of the few PHAs around with an EIS diploma and a Watney's Red Barrel, the symbol of being an EIS graduate.

Grade Has Its Privileges

In 1968, the Centers for Disease Control (CDC) had a National Immunization Conference in San Diego, California, at the El Cortez Hotel. This was the first time I remember staying in a hotel where the elevator shaft was transparent and partly outside the building. This allowed you to see the inside beauty of the hotel and outside scenery as you used it. The scenery in San Diego was magnificent. This was the first city that I had ever seen where all the utilities were underground. Therefore, there was no unsightly poles to distract from the natural beauty. It was a very clean city and with marvelous structures and foliage everywhere. The climate at this time of year was outstanding and certainly more temperate than where most of the conference attendees came from.

The conference featured presentations by immunization experts from national, state, and local programs. It was great to be there and to meet some of the experts on vaccine preventable diseases. It was my first real exposure to these leading physicians, scientists, and program managers. The information was interesting and really more than one could absorb at one time.

Several of the junior public health advisors who attended the CDC's EIS Course in Atlanta earlier in the year were there and we as a group hung out together. After all these years I don't remember all of them, but I do remember Bill Pack, Jim Thompson, and Louie Spruill. We noticed that some of our senior public health advisors, the CDC state representatives, had shed their coats and ties and had become more casual. Prominent among these Senor PHAs was Larry Dodd and Ray Overton. The dress code for CDC public health advisors at this time was that we wore coats and ties at all work and official functions. Therefore, this was an indication that if they could go casual that we could do the same. After all we were in San Diego. Therefore, at the next conference function we came in our casual dress. We certainly were a lot more comfortable and really more receptive to the material being presented. At the break, we as a group were approached by our CDC regional representative, Jack Benson, and were told in a firm, but diplomatic manner that we needed to wear coats and ties. We with no discussion complied to Jack's strong suggestion. However, the senior PHA's from our region continued to dress casually. This was our first exposure to the mantra that rank has its privileges.

Raccoon Hunting: A Different Kind of Sport

During the time I was assigned by the Centers for Disease Control and Prevention (CDC) to the Mississippi Immunization Program, Glen Collins was assigned as the CDC's state representative for the Mississippi Venereal Disease Program. Glen and his wife, Carol, and Jane, my wife, and I became friends. One of our main outings was going to various restaurants in the Jackson area. Our favorite restaurant was Conestoga's Steak House near the dam on the Ross Barnett Reservoir. The steaks were magnificent and the baked potatoes were the size of footballs.

Glen was a hunter and his favorite sport was raccoon hunting. Many nights Glen would hunt all night. With little sleep, he would come to work early and put in a full day in the office. The next night, he would go hunting again. Glen was without question quite a man on all levels. I remember that one night he took Del Hammons, CDC's Regional Director, hunting and completely wore him out. This was a man that had been in the Marine Corps during World War II.

Glen taught me a great deal about coon hunting. The most important part of hunting is having a well-trained dog. Glen spent many hours training dogs and hunting with them in different locations, including some pretty rugged swamps. In my opinion, there were some creatures in the swamp I didn't want to be around, especially at night. One training device was an electrical collar that would lightly shock a dog when it started chasing any animal other than a raccoon. Glen had one dog he called Boomerang. When I asked him why he named the dog Boomerang, this is the story he told me. The dog took a long time to train and was not always obedient. After much effort, Glen got the dog to be a pretty good coon dog. During competitive hunts, Boomerang would be the first to strike the scent of the raccoon and the first to tree one. These are important qualities and they gain many valuable points for the hunter. As a result, Glen won a lot of championships. This means money and trophies. Every hunter wants the best dog and is willing to pay a high price for a quality animal. Many hunters wanted to buy Boomerang. Glen would tell them that his dog would only hunt for him. After a while they would offer a price that he couldn't refuse. After a period of time, the hunter would complain to Glen that the dog wouldn't hunt for him. Glen would remind them what he had told them prior to buying Boomerang. Glen would offer to buy the dog back for a much smaller price. This happened three time in a row. Each time Glen made several hundred dollars. Therefore, Glen's coon dog became Boomerang. The fourth time, the dog was bought by a breeder from Indiana and Glen never saw Boomerang ever again.

Glen received some notoriety in Mississippi and Alabama for importing and selling some small mules. I believe he bought the mules in

Oklahoma. On raccoon hunts, hunters could ride the small mules rather than walk. The mules being shorter made them more practical as they were capable of traveling under low-lying tree branches. This was particularly important since hunting is done at night. More ground could be covered faster and with less wear and tear on the body. Another feature, the small mules were trained to jump small fences. You could lay a blanket over the fence and the mule would jump to other side. Once a hunter saw what the Oklahoma mule could do, they wanted one. I do know Glen imported and sold a lot of mules. Glen loved the sport and was able to pay for the hobby by selling dogs and mules.

I went with Glen one time and one time was enough. Raccoon hunting is a different sport that takes a great deal of time, endurance, and skill.

Choctaw County Hunting

I have been hunting before I was a teenager. I started hunting with a friend of my daddy's, Mike Hipp, and his son Bobby. They taught me to hunt squirrels, birds, and particularly ducks. Eventually, I began hunting deer with my friend Henry Hixson and his father, Tom. Since my daddy didn't hunt, these special friends made it possible for me to become a hunter and love the outdoors. It is something that I still love to do in my senior years. Jane and I now live on Cold Mountain in the Blue Ridge Mountains. We live here because we love the mountains and the outdoors. Some of the reasons that we are here goes back to my many years of hunting.

When we got to Mississippi, the amount of hunting and the type of hunting in which I participated increased several times over. This was because of a man that I worked with in Mississippi named Kenneth Bruce. His family along with other Choctaw County families came from Fairfield County, South Carolina, in the early 19th century. Bruce knew everyone in the county including the former Mississippi

Governor, JP Coleman. From the first time I hunted with Kenneth, I fell in love with the county and the people. Those who hunted with me treated me like family.

We hunted deer on a regular basis and harvested many deer. Together we had more than enough venison to go around. We hunted with dogs. This to me is the most fun of all the types of deer hunting experienced. Hunters are set up on roads surrounding an area where deer bed or a swamp where deer are known to stay. For safety, hunters are spaced at a minimum of 100-yards apart. Then a driver releases the dogs, mostly red tick and blue tick hounds. When the dogs strike deer scent, every hunter knows it from the barking. When the dogs jump a deer, the barking intensifies and becomes louder. Every hunter with the heart beating out of their chest prepares himself for what he hopes will be the presence of a large buck. On most hunts we harvested at least one nice animal. We hunted almost every weekend during deer season. This was to Jane's chagrin. She was left home with our sons. Over time, Jane and the boys would come with me on occasion and they would stay with Bruce's mother and sister while we hunted.

The other type of hunting Bruce exposed me to was quail hunting. Although I had done some quail hunting when I was young, this was at another level. He raised pointers and setters and he had trained them well. In the morning we would hunt with two pointers and in the afternoon, we would hunt with a pair of setters, or vice versa. On most hunts, we would kill our limit. The dogs would find a covey of quail and then we would flush them and usually kill two or three birds as they scattered. Then we would hunt the singles. The nice thing about hunting with him was property lines were no boundary. We would just climb or breach the fence and kept on hunting. His neighbors had already given permission for us to hunt their land. Climbing the fences were problematic for me, but not for Bruce. He was six-feet three inches tall and I was barely five-feet ten inches. At the end of the day, we would have a mess of quail. I learned quickly not to argue with Ms. Bruce, Kenneth's mother. She would always clean the quail and place them in a milk carton for me to take home. The first time I complained about her cleaning the birds, she emphatically said, "I cleaned quail for my husband and I will clean them for my son and his friends." From the first time I hunted with Kenneth, Mrs. Bruce dressed the quail. If you have never eaten quail, you are missing something. I would rather eat quail than chicken anytime.

A sad side story was that all of Bruce's dogs were killed one off season. As I mentioned earlier, he had numerous trained bird dogs. Because he needed a large amount of dog food, he would buy it in bulk from a feed store nearby. For some unknown reason, the feed was laced with some form of rat poison. Every dog died. It took him a very long time to obtain new dogs and train them. It also took an inordinately long time to procure a settlement from the feed company.

I was privileged to go dove hunting with Bruce and many of his Weir friends on a regular basis. Another close friend who worked with Kenneth and me, Paul Dykes, would also join us on occasion. One year, Dr. Barney Cottrell, the Mississippi State Health Director, joined us for a hunt. In fact, he rode with me to Weir. He had a great time. They would grow grains and harvest them right before dove season. On the first day of the dove season, we would all have a designated area with safe distance from another hunter. At noon, the start of the dove hunt, the sky must have looked like it did at Pearl Harbor, dove would be flying everywhere. The field sounded like a war zone. Most hunts would result in numerous doves being harvested and cleaned. Of course, when we got home, they made for good eating. By the way, I did clean my own dove.

All the hunting described above was a phenomenal experience. I learned a great deal from Kenneth Bruce and his Choctaw County friends. We remain friends after all these years even though we have not seen each other in person for over two decades. This is another memory that I will always cherish. On many hunting trips I would stay with the Bruce family. On some of my trips, Jane and the boys would join me. The meals that Mrs. Bruce and her daughter, Elsie, would prepare for us were fantastic. She would have a couple of different meats, several vegetables, rice and gravy, homemade biscuits, and a couple of desserts. If I was there for breakfast, it would be both hearty and abundant. It goes without saying, the Bruce family will always have a special place in our hearts. Choctaw County hunting and hospitality were special in numerous ways.

Need a Drink and a Rape Crisis Center

After several years in the first house that we owned, we decided to buy a new and bigger home in a better area of Jackson. There was a number of reasons for our decision. First, our family had grown to four and we needed a larger home. Secondly, we could afford a better home. Third, the present area had deteriorated over the last year or two. Fourth, the quality of the education at the school across from our home had regressed. I believe you are getting the jest of what I am saying. We were ready for a move.

We started looking for a new home and found a new subdivision that was being built. In contacting the main builder, we found a lot and a floor plan that we liked. Then we signed a contract and placed earnest money to have the house built. Jane would basically be able to select siding, lighting, paints, framing, cabinets, appliances, etc. From the time the house was started, we monitored progress almost daily. We would see errors or omissions and the superintendent would make corrections. Often this was done after heated discussions between Jane and the builder. He tried to tell her what she needed or wanted. Wrong thing to do. Jane has always had a mind of her own. The builder actually had a heart attack and died about the time the house was completed. I have often kidded her that she was responsible for his heart attack.

As the house was being built, we put the old house on the market. The old house sold about the same time the new house was ready for occupancy. This created the need to have two house closings almost simultaneously. This is when you learn the hard way the real world of real estate and mortgages. During the closings, a check would be written to the Realtor; then a check was written to the bank; another check was written to the closing attorney; and another check was written to the builder, etc. In other words, it appeared everyone was taking our money, in all the transactions. At the end of the day, we received less money for our old house than we expected and we paid out far more than we expected for our new house.

When the day was over Jane was a bundle of nerves. Although Jane has never been a drinker, I stopped at the nearest liquor store and bought her a canned mixed drink. After a few gulps, she calmed down. We both agreed that closings make you feel like you have been raped. We both felt like we needed to go to a Rape Crisis Center.

A positive side of selling our old home was the overall financial outcome. After doing the math, we were very pleased by the bottom line. When we calculated our capital gains and added what we recouped on the tax deductions for interest paid on our mortgage and property taxes, we found that we had lived six years at the old property free and made an additional $3000. Pretty darn good return on our investment. Then when viewed from the standpoint of what we would have lost by renting, the financial difference was staggering. From this point forward, we would invest in a larger and better home each time we moved. The return each time was amazing. One reason for the financial stability that we enjoy today can be associated with our real estate investments.

One side board to the above stories is having our furniture and belongings moved from the old house to the new house. A friend in the Jaycees family owned a moving company. He gave us a good deal for an in-town move. The deal did not work out for either of us. His team of movers worked with speed at the detriment to our furniture. When they finished, they had done a number on our limited furniture. It goes without saying, he owed us more than he made. The repairs were not cheap. A good deal was not so great for either of us.

The Volkswagen That Wasn't Economical

Even though I got a nice promotion the year after we moved to Mississippi, Jane and I were still not living high on the hog. We had two young sons and now living on one income. We had lived on two incomes before we left South Carolina. We had a beautiful 1967 Pontiac LeMans that we both loved. It was powerful and a good open road car, but it gave bad gas mileage. As I was traveling a great deal on business, it was impacting our financial bottom line. Jane and I made the decision to trade the Pontiac in on a 1969 Volkswagen Squareback. It was like a modern SUV with plenty of room for the four of us plus our luggage. It gave much better gas mileage and therefore we were initially very pleased. This vehicle served me well in transporting supplies to the Mississippi Gulf Coast during Hurricane Camille. In about a year after Camille, I was coming back from Vicksburg, when smoke began bellowing out of the exhaust pipe. At first it was a shock and then it became apparent that there was a major problem. I pulled over at the first service station and made arrangements to have the Squareback towed to the Volkswagen dealership in Jackson. Then I made arrangements for a loaner and went home in despair. The next day the service department called and informed me that a valve had overheated and blown. The good news was the valve was covered under warranty. They also informed me that a second valve may have warped and did I want it replaced while the engine was disassembled. In the long run, it would be cheaper for us. Jane and I agree to have them do the other valve at our expense. Add the towing charges, rental car expenses, and the valve replacement, it was obvious the savings that we had envisioned when we bought the Squareback had just evaporated.

Zoom forward 18 months to December, the four of us were happy to be heading to South Carolina for Christmas. Close to Meridian, the Volkswagen starting blowing blue smoke out of the tailpipe. We had the car towed in to the local Volkswagen dealership. Initial evaluation was that at least one valve had blown. We were dejected on two fronts. First, the Squareback was down a second time and how much would it cost us. Secondly, it looked like Christmas at South Carolina was out of the question. We called home with the bad news. In less than an hour, we received a call from my daddy telling us that he and Jane's mother, Lavinia Miller, were coming to get us. They drove all night long and picked the four of us up along with our luggage and Christmas gifts. Our spirits soared. We informed the dealership what was happening and gave them a number where we could be reached. Now the silver lining, when we got to Columbia my "Mimi" Boykin decided that she didn't want to drive anymore and agreed to sell us Pop Boykin's almost new 1968 Plymouth Valiant for $1500. My pop had recently passed away. We readily agreed. This would give us a second car which we badly needed and this would also give us a vehicle to return to Meridian after Christmas. Then came even better news. The dealership called and informed us the Volkswagen would be fixed at their expense. The Squareback should have been recalled and a vent kit installed to make sure the engine didn't over-heat. During manufacture, the original air vents had been installed incorrectly and this was why our valves were being blown. A bad start to Christmas had ended on a high note.

"The rest of the story," as Paul Harvey would have said. About a year later at a routine checkup, we were informed that another valve was getting ready to go. With very little discussion, we made a decision to trade cars. We traded for an almost new Plymouth Fury. It had been a demonstrator that the dealership had used. This became Jane's least favorite car of all the ones that we have ever owned. Of course, this is another whole story. The Volkswagen Squareback that was bought to save money was a pain in the posterior.

Me and Elvis

During my time as a Jackson, Mississippi Jaycee, I attended the U.S. Jaycees Outstanding Young Men in America Ceremony in Nashville, Tennessee. Ten outstanding individuals were selected to be recognized from all over this great country. Each person under 36 years of age had accomplished a great deal at a young age. I don't remember all their names, but I do remember Elvis Presley and Ron Zeigler, President Nixon's press secretary. As it happened, I was among the Jaycees in Elvis Presley's entourage. On the day of his recognition, our job was to accompany him in and out of the auditorium. We met him at his chauffeured Rolls-Royce and led him into an anteroom near the podium. This was accomplished in a dignified manner with very little fanfare. After a few minutes of banter with him, it was time for his ceremony. He was brought on to the platform and then he was introduced and his numerous achievements highlighted, many of which were outside of his role as an entertainer. I remember especially his involvement with law enforcement. President Nixon had given him an official badge from one law enforcement agency. I believe it was the Drug Enforcement Agency (DEA). Elvis accepted the award and then spoke for some time about how much the award meant to him and how he loved our great country. It goes without saying, this was the most packed session in the weekend event. It was standing room only. Now we took him back to his car. Remember, now the Jaycees and their wives or girlfriends knew Elvis was present. As we left the convention center by the back door, there were hundreds of people, mainly women, circling his Rolls-Royce. Some were in the car taking any and everything, including match stems and cigar butts from the ashtrays. Remember, these were not teenagers, these were grown women. Police had to clear them away for us to get him to the car. People tried to touch him, kiss him, and heaven knows what else. This was my first experience seeing close up what a genuine Superstar has to go through routinely. No wonder Elvis was involved in some unorthodox behavior to try an escape.

As a side story, at another session, I was sitting near the VIP section and heard a familiar voice. I turned and sitting near me was George Herbert Walker Bush. He was the U.S. Ambassador to the United Nations and later President of the United States. I shook his hand and told him how good it was to meet him. He was a very nice man and most cordial. What you saw, was what you got.

The Real Buford Pusser of *Walking Tall* Fame

During my term as president of the Jackson Jaycees, I was attending the Mississippi Jaycees State Convention in Tupelo, Mississippi. One of the featured speakers was Buford Pusser, the legendary McNairy County, Tennessee, sheriff who had taken on the Dixie Mafia. This group ran illegal gambling, prostitution rings, and drug enterprises in north Mississippi and southern Tennessee. It actually became a war between the two factions. Buford eventually cleaned up the area. In the process he was beat up and severely knifed and his wife was murdered by the Dixie Mafia. Because of his fame, a book was written about him and a movie, *Walking Tall*, was produced about his life. Buford was at the Jaycee convention to promote the movie. He was not the star in the movie, but the real character and the subject of the movie. Eventually a sequel to the movie would be produced.

At a cocktail party, I was able to meet Buford and for some unknown reason to me, we struck up a friendship. He let me hold his large bat that he had created to fight the Mafia. He preferred the bat to a firearm. I understood that with his size that the bat was a force to be reckoned with. After the convention, we remained in touch with each other. He knew that I was conducting immunization campaigns throughout the state. Therefore, if he was going to be in Mississippi, he would call me and we would meet for a meal and sometimes for drinks. One night I was in Clarkston when he called to let me know he was in Cleveland nearby and wanted to know if I would come for supper and drinks. I agreed and a few of my staff rode with me to meet Buford. The fact is they would have walked to Cleveland to meet him. After supper, we all went to the bar next door. Word got out that Buford Pusser, the legend, was in town. It looked like every female in the Delta came to the bar. They all wanted to meet the man. Kenneth Bruce, my supervisor for North Mississippi, and I were appointed by Buford to keep order and screen the women. They came in all shapes, sizes, ages. They wanted autographs, to sit on his lap, and only heaven knows what else. Buford did not have movie star looks. As a former professional wrestler, he was strongly built and weighed about 250 pounds. For over two hours, the fans kept coming. It taxed the ability of Kenneth and me to keep order. Because we were with Buford, we also became targets. Without a doubt this was one of the most interesting evenings that I ever remember. Fame and fortune create a hysteria that few people seldom see.

Buford and I kept up our friendship for a few more years. Then I got transferred to Texas and we went separate ways. At some point, I heard that Buford had been killed. It appears someone tampered with the brakes on his car and he was killed in a bad car wreck. The implication was that the Dixie Mafia had gotten their revenge, but I don't know whether that was ever proven.

A Decade of Tornado Experiences

For a decade in living in Mississippi and Texas, as a family we had more involvement with tornadoes than during all our years growing up in South Carolina. The number of tornadoes experienced annually in Mississippi dwarfs anything we have seen in the other states where we have lived.

The first tornado that I remember hit at night and was totally without warning. Jane woke me from a sound sleep and informed me that there was a loud roar outside that sounded like a train. She also said debris was hitting the house. My response was that it was just a thunderstorm and it would soon be over. Then I rolled over and went back to sleep. In the morning, it was obvious that it had been a tornado. It came down the street bordering our house and the elementary school across the street. Both structures had been spared. However, many homes in our community had been damaged or destroyed. The phenomena had jumped all around and gyrated up and down. Our home had been spared by luck or some divine power. Whatever it was, we were very thankful.

The second tornado hit while we were on a family drive to the Ross Barnett Reservoir. We were crossing the dam when we saw coming across the lake a very dark cloud. We started to feel the wind and rain, hear the thunder, and see lightning. There was absolutely nowhere we could go. On one side of the dam was the deep lake and the other side was a drop-off of several hundred feet. I stopped the car and waited. We were soon wrapped in the dark cloud and the car started to shake. After what seemed forever, the cloud was past us. With relief we drove to the other side of the dam. Then we turned around and drove back home. Later, we found out that what we had been involved in was a tornado. Then it dawned on me what might have happened. Our car could have been hurled into the lake or down the steep hill. Neither scenario would have been good. Again, someone was watching over us.

In one night, Mississippi encountered more than 100 tornadoes. The television station was constantly barking out warnings. The warning would say up front that this is not a watch. A tornado is on the ground at Raymond heading northeast. A tornado is now in Clinton and moving southwest. This went on for hours. Jane stayed inside and gave us updates as I and some of our neighbors watched the sky for hours. Yes, we saw some funnels that thankfully didn't come down. I believe this is one of the most anxious nights that I ever remember. The next morning the news was reported that the towns of Little Yazoo, Cary, and Inverness had literally had been destroyed and there had been many fatalities. I don't remember the exact number, but I think it was around 100 deaths. A night like this one, shows you how fragile life can be and that nothing should ever be taken for granted.

The last tornado in Mississippi that I remember was while I was at work. My office was several miles from our residence. Another afternoon for tornado watches and warnings was in place and the skies in my area were sinister-looking. I had walked outside to observe the sky for the second time when the warning sirens went off. This meant a tornado has been observed and to find shelter. I saw the black cloud that was indicative of a tornado. I ran back inside and notified my staff to find a safe place to protect themselves. Soon the cloud was past us and the twister had not touched the ground. Now as I looked out the window, the tornado was headed in the direction toward our home. My heart jumped out of my body. God be with my family. I called Jane and received no answer. My anxiety grew. After what I thought was forever, Jane called to let me know that she, Paul III, and Robert were fine. She had sheltered in the closet. The twister went directly over our house. Thank God the family was safe. Our only loss was the television antennae, our grill, and a few other expendable yard items.

The first tornado that we experienced in Texas was in my vegetable garden and the green belt next to our lot. From our experiences, Jane and I knew it was a tornado. The tornadic action of the winds was symptomatic. Certainly, it wasn't close to what we had seen in Mississippi, but it could do some damage. Jane called the television station to notify the weather anchor what was happening. The first statement out of his mouth was, "Where are you from?" When she said Mississippi, he said that she was right. They were tracking a tornado on radar that was in the Round Rock area. He was from Mississippi and he understood what we had seen too. Seems the people in Austin were not very savvy about tornadoes.

The last story about tornadoes in Texas was during a Little League Baseball game. The team for which I was one of the coaches was playing our game. Out of nowhere came a significant storm similar to the ones I had seen in Mississippi. The umpire stopped the game until the storm passed. Fans, coaches, and players wanted to finish the game. As we all stood there watching the storm approach, I knew what we were seeing. I could see the spout among the dark clouds. I told the crowd what I had seen and knew. I advised that we all needed to go to safety quickly. A few argued that we should wait out the storm. My response was, "You can stay, but my family and my team are out of here." Yes, it was a tornado. I might add that when we left, the majority followed us.

The above experiences make Jane and me very conscience of bad weather and we are ready to take quick action if necessary. God helps those who help themselves. Thank goodness, tornadoes in the Blue Ridge Mountains where we now live are very rare.

The Best Hunting Boot Ever

Prior to being transferred from Mississippi to Texas, I had a thank-you party for my staff at Jane's and my home. This group of men and women had helped me run immunization campaigns in every county in Mississippi. They were responsible for immunizing tens of thousands of children for measles and rubella. I was happy to have supervised such a great staff. My thanks to them was a very small token for what they accomplished.

As a going-away present, they gave me a pair of Browning hunting boots and a pair of hunting pants with the legs covered in leather. These pants would protect me from briars when I quail hunted. Both were thoughtful gifts that were very practical and useful. The pants wore out many years ago. However, the Browning hunting boots, although not the originals, are still with me today. After moving from Texas to Georgia, I continued to deer hunt and the Browning boots were still used regularly. In the mid-1980s, on one hunt the sole on one of the boots separated. This appeared highly unusual. Since Browning boots are very expensive and are guaranteed, I notified the Browning Company about the problem. They sent me a new pair just like the original. How is that for living up to your warranty?

After moving to North Carolina in 2003, the same thing happened again. It just happened that the Browning Boot Factory was then in Morganton, NC. I returned the boots with an accompanying letter. Guess what? They no longer made the original boot, but they sent me a catalog and coupon worth up to $225 toward a new pair. The pair of Browning boots that I selected cost $15 more than the coupon. As a result, the Browning boots I was given by my staff in 1974, are still being used in 2021. A gift, like a Timex watch, that keeps on ticking. When I use the boots, I often think of the great people I worked with in the Mississippi Immunization Program. Some are still my friends after all these years.

My Precious Cat Is Dead

Growing up, I had a dog name Smut from the time I was a toddler until I was a sophomore in college. This is my way of saying that I was a dog person. I didn't have anything against cats, but nobody in my family and, as far as I know, none of my friends had cats. This all changed when I married Jane. Her family had dogs and cats. Therefore, at some point cats became a part of our family.

Jane had a Manx given to her. At least that is what I think it was called. This was a cat of cats. It had large and strong legs and could jump like a rabbit. You could throw a ball in the air and the cat would catch the ball six or seven feet off the floor. Another time our son, Paul III, found stray kittens beside the road and brought them home. When I was relaxing in my La-Z-Boy, the little balls of fur were placed in my lap. You are right without discussion, we kept them. In Mississippi, a stray cat, Tom, adopted us. He was a survivor. One time, the Pearl River flooded and the creek in back of our house became a river. Tom had gone prowling and got stranded on the other side of the river. Weeks went by without Tom's presence and therefore the family thought he was gone forever. Then one night I was working in my garden and, in the distance, I saw something white. It was Tom coming home. He had survived six weeks in the wild. We eventually took him with us to Texas. With the exception of him staking his claim on our small apartment near the University of Texas, he was a good and docile animal. After our home was built in the northwest hills, Tom enjoyed roaming the wilderness area near home. Then he disappeared and never returned. We conjured up many scenarios about what could have happened to him, but we never had evidence of what might have really happened.

The above elongated explanation is to give you an understanding that the Turner family was a cat family. At some point someone gave us a cat that we named Patches. Patches was gray with patches of white, therefore you understand how he got his name. He had a personality like no cat we ever had. The two of us bonded immediately. This was our first cat that I considered mine. We played together and I loved stroking him and hearing him purr. When I would go into the garden, he would follow me. At some point, he climbed up my pants wanting me to put him on my shoulders. Where he would remain while I worked in the vegetable garden. From this point on, Patches was on my shoulder when I was working in the garden. Jane and the boys would laugh and smile when they saw this sight. This is to demonstrate that I really loved Patches and he loved me.

Jon and Beryl Snelling came to visit us from Mississippi. Jon who was with the Department for Defense was going to San Antonio to interview for a job. Our two families did the tourist thing and as always had a great time together. At some point I was walking out of the garage and Patches came after me. Jon simultaneously was shutting the garage door. The door came down on Patches neck. His neck was broken and he died instantly. I was absolutely devasted. This was a creature that I loved with all my heart. The whole family loved this special animal. I don't think I was civil to Jon and I probably blamed him for what happened. Looking back Jon wouldn't have hurt Patches for anything.

The next day, Jane, Paul III, Robert, and I placed Patches into a shoe box and took him to a vacant lot and buried him. The boys placed some his favorite items into the box before placing it in the grave. Then, we had a brief ceremony and a prayer. My sweet and precious Patches was gone, but his memory lives on.

Le Richelieu: What a Headquarters

The state of Louisiana Immunization Program was having a major rubella immunization campaign and needed help for the massive endeavor. The CDC Regional Office in Dallas called and asked me if I would go to New Orleans from Austin to help them manage the campaign. Of course, I was happy to respond positively to their request. When I arrived at the Le Richelieu Hotel where I was staying, I found in addition to a large contingent of Louisiana personnel from all parts of the state, several other fellow CDC employees present. After all these years, I can't remember everyone, but I do remember Luther DeWeese, Don Stenhouse, Dr. Phil Landrigan. Luther was from the Dallas Regional Office and Don and Phil were from CDC Headquarters in Atlanta.

Since the immunization campaign would last several days, the Le Richelieu management gave us the penthouse to use for our headquarters. It probably would be of interest that the day we took over the penthouse, Lee Majors, the movie and television star, checked out. It was exciting to be in a suite where the rich and famous usually resided. The Le Richelieu Hotel was a regal old hotel that was built in the French style and was a prominent fixture in the French quarter very near Jackson Square. If the facility could talk, what history it could tell. You could actually feel the spirits of the past all around you. It was decided quickly that the penthouse would not only serve as our headquarters, it would serve as the location for our hospitality hour and our evening meals. This was driven by the knowledge that one of the members in the Louisiana team had been a master sergeant in the U.S. Army and served as a master chef in embassies around the world. We would give Fontenau money in the morning as we departed and when we returned in the evening, he would have a feast prepared. This included iced-down beer and wine. I remember one particular meal that was, in my opinion, by far our best meal. Fontenau had prepared chicken-sauce-picante, a magnificent salad, and hot French bread. I can still smell the aroma and remember the exquisite taste after all these years. Never before had I eaten so well within the federal per diem.

Each night before dinner we would have a stellar cocktail hour to unwind after the rigors of the day. Fontenau always waited until we all had eaten before he ate his meal. The night we had chicken-sauce-picante, as he ate, a chicken bone got lodged in his throat. Dr. Phil Landrigan was the only doctor nearby. Phil had really enjoyed the adult beverages and was very relaxed not drunk. Upon being called, Phil became very alert and immediately assisted Fontenau in his distress. Phil accompanied our chef to the hospital. To our relief the next morning he was back and fine. Another great meal was on the menu for the night meal.

The rubella campaign in New Orleans was a great success with many thousands of young people being immunized. However, the camaraderie and meals at the Le Richelieu were the highlight of the week.

An Opportunity or a Scam

When we lived in Austin, we were very fortunate to have lived in a very lovely and friendly neighborhood, Balcones Woods. As a result, we did a lot of activities together. There was swimming at the pool, tennis at the tennis courts, a bridge club, etc. Some of our neighbors who had boats regularly invited us to go to the lake with them. On one of these trips, one neighbor invited John and Dell Gully and us to become partners in an oil exploration. In other words, for what I believe was $5000, we could become partners in an oil well exploration with a percentage of the profits should we strike oil. John and

I discussed the opportunity and explored risk and benefits. We both decided to become involved in the venture which was in the Abilene area. We signed the necessary paperwork and anted up our money. After several months we were notified that the company had struck oil and the grade of oil was so good they didn't even have to do a stem test. The volume of oil should result in a very healthy return. The good news placed me in a heavenly mood. A couple months later the same neighbor presented me with a second opportunity to invest in a second well. Why not? The return from the first well would protect me from any major loss. Some of my public health advisor friends, Glen Collins and George Palmer, decided to also invest based on what had happened in the first venture. Jane's first cousin, Barbara Allen, who was visiting us also decided to invest in the second venture. My enthusiasm generated from the success of the first well sucked those around me into investing in the second well.

Now the rest of the story, as Paul Harvey would say. Several months later I was notified that the first oil well had gone dry. The second well never produced any oil at all. The Turner family went from the mountaintop to the valley. Although we got a little money back and the oil deletion allowance saved us some money on our taxes, we lost a good sum of money. What was going to be a boom, became a bust. John Gully and I discussed what had happened and really believed that we had been scammed. The oil company lost nothing one way or the other. They had all the money they needed up front. If they drilled a dry hole, they lost nothing. If they struck oil, they would use it to promote another drilling operation. We speculated that even if a well was successful, they would say at some point that it had gone dry and one of their subcompanies would buy the well at pennies on the dollar. Then at some time in the future, the old well would be reactivated. The poor investors were always the losers. People with deep pockets would benefit from the oil depletion allowance, more than me and my friends. It might not have been a scam, but John and I thought it probably was. My biggest regret was that my excitement resulted in others being pulled into their net. From that day forward, I took the stance that if it sounds too good to be true, it probably is. It should be mentioned, that this kind of speculation was a contributing factor to banks in Texas going upside down. People borrowed money to invest in oil speculation and then when the ventures tanked, they couldn't pay back their loans.

My story made me think about the story of my friends, Don Stenhouse's, father-in-law, Tex Maddox. Mr. Maddox invested handsomely in a franchise called Minnie Pearl Fried Chicken. The venture crashed and burned. Tex was mayor of Lebanon, Tennessee, and some of his friends wanted him to invest in a new business, Cracker Barrel. I believe the investment would have been $10,000, a sizable amount at the time. Remembering what had happened earlier, he declined. What a return he would have had if he had invested in Cracker Barrel.

Tex and I both were burned one time and that probably prevented us from investing in other successful opportunities.

A United Methodist That Acted Like a Roman Catholic

When we lived in Austin, Texas, our subdivision, Balcones Woods, was the friendliest and closest neighborhood in which we ever had the privilege to live. On our street was the Bob Kubichek family that belonged to a nearby Roman Catholic church. On several occasions, they invited us to attend a family event that was being held for their parish. It included many activities for the whole family. One event that I particularly enjoyed was a horse racing venue where you were given sheets to evaluate horses and then place bets on the pending race. Betting was just like you were at a real racetrack. You could make a bet on a horse to win or place. You could bet on a perfecto. In other words, you could make a number of different bets as there was a number of different combinations. By the way, bets were made with real money, but the maximum on any one bet was $2. After all bets were made, a video of an actual race would be run. Then, the winning tickets would be rewarded with a real payout. The church kept a percentage of the money from each race. The racing event manger had to be good at math or at least good at reading the event instructions. It was a great deal of fun and I enjoyed it immensely. By the way, unlike United Methodists, they sold adult beverages during the festivities. After attending several of these family affairs, the parish priest came over to me and engaged me in conversation. After learning that I was a Methodist, he stated that, "I partied like a good Catholic." My thoughts were that I was glad my staunch Southern Baptist grandparents, Granddaddy and Nanny Turner, were not anywhere in the vicinity. In reflection, I think my Catholic friends take to heart the words of Jesus Christ that say it is not what you eat or drink that defiles you, but what is in your heart.

A Close Neighborhood That Enjoyed Life

When we lived in Austin, we had a very close neighborhood. Balcones Woods was a new subdivision and most of the families were young with the average age being around 35. Several families were military and with the father, an officer, serving at Bergstrom Air Force Base. Others of us were career civil service managers. Then we had a number of young executives with IBM and Texas Instruments. Most families were there only for a short time before they would be transferred. Therefore, we all became close quickly. Some of us were in a bridge club that included having a meal and playing bridge at a different home every month. Several of us played tennis together on a regular basis and eventually played on a competitive team in an area league. Our children swam together at the pool in our subdivision and some of the children swam on a competitive swim team that competed all over Austin. You can see that there was great opportunity for togetherness. Out of these friendships grew additional opportunities to enjoy events and experiences together.

We would ice down beer and soft drinks and several carloads of us would trek the 40 miles to the small town of Elgin. Some of us would enjoy drinking beer on the way. It was legal in Texas to drink and drive. Then we would enjoy barbeque at Copeland's Barbeque. The meal would include brisket, ribs, sausage, and all the trimmings. After dinner, we would go next door to the old-timey saloon and dance. We made this trip on a regular basis. Every trip was an adventure and entertainment of the first order.

On another occasion we rented a bus and took a trip to the Wurst Festival at New Braunfels. We partied down and back as well as while we were there. There was plenty of German beer and food. Of course, there were polka bands everywhere. I remember that beer was served in long beer steins. All lines for beer were long and crowded. Once you got your stein, you had to maneuver back to your table. Between what you drank on the way to your table and what you spilled because of the crowd, when you got back to your seat the stein was almost empty. Therefore, you would have to start the process all over again. The trip and event were greatly enjoyed by all us who participated.

Austin back then hosted each year an Aqua Festival that lasted a full week. Each day one of Texas' ethnic groups would be featured. Foods, dances, and costumes for that ethic background would be featured, for example: German, Czechoslovakian, Mexican, etc. Each night was different and therefore a different experience. During the week they would have boat races on Lake Austin. Groups from our neighborhood would go the Aqua Festival nightly.

It goes without further elaboration that the Balcones Woods neighborhood was special in many ways and will never be forgotten. We have stayed in touch with some of these neighbors over the years.

Profound Loss of a Friend

While we were in Austin, Texas, we made friends with a couple in our subdivision, Mike and Jan Wagner. They lived just down the street from us and were parents of three wonderful children. We socialized together. We went to the same church and were in the same Sunday school class. Our sons played baseball in the same league. As a result, we were around each other often. I remember they ran Davis' nursery which had been started by Jan's parents. This business and their children kept them very busy. Although the couple was very busy and involved with family, they were fun to be around. In my opinion, the star that shined brightest in this family was Jan. She was beautiful inside and out. Her radiant smile was genuine and when she talked to you her eyes appeared to sparkle. She was a great mother and her children were the center of her universe. She was always taking her children somewhere.

Suffice is to say this was one of the couples we hated to leave when we transferred to Atlanta. We would keep in touch with the Wagner family. On visits to Austin, we would always see the family. One night as we were getting ready to go out for the evening, we received a call from Dell Gully. She told us that Jan had been killed in a car wreck. The breath was sucked out of both of us. I could clearly see Jan and her beautiful smile and sparkling eyes. I am seeing them clearly this morning as I write this story. What a loss this was to Mike and their three children. What a loss this was to their many friends.

The way Jan died was horrific. The entrance to Balcones Woods subdivision was on Highway 183. As more subdivisions and businesses were built in the area, the highway became extremely busy. As a result, a new stoplight was installed at the entrance to the subdivision. One day Jan was called from the school, I think the school was Pillow Elementary, notifying her that her son was sick and needed to be picked up. Jan immediately headed to the school. As she pulled into the intersection at the new traffic light, a dump truck ran the stop light and T-boned Jan's car. Jan was killed instantly. One of the sweetest and prettiest people Jane and I have ever known was gone too soon. The loss to the family was devasting. The joy Jan created to those around her had evaporated instantly and it would take years for them to recover.

I now communicate with Jan's daughter, Kim, on Facebook. I have told her before about what I have just written here about her mother. Isn't it amazing how a person in a short time can impact your life? Rest in peace Jan Wagner. You are gone, but you will never be forgotten.

Can I Speak to "Buster" Turner?

At one time in my life, I was the President of the Atlanta Gamecock Club. In fact, I was president for five years. As a result, I was also a member of the University of South Carolina Gamecock Club Board of Directors in Columbia, SC. My Eau Claire High School Coach, Art Baker, became an Associate Athletic Director at the University of South Carolina and the Director of the Gamecock Club. When I attended board meetings, the coach and I enjoyed being together and reminiscing about times together in Eau Claire. Coach went to College Place Methodist with my family and we knew a lot of the same people. Therefore, we always had a lot of catching up to do. It was ironic that the Associate Director of the Gamecock Club, Herb Sharp, had graduated from Eau Claire and had been my wife, Jane's, next- door neighbor. All that is to demonstrate that my relationship to them was different from most of the other Board Members. At most board meetings, we would visit before and after the meetings. Art felt comfortable to bounce pending issues off me to get my thoughts and advice.

One day he needed my counsel on some issue and he called my office. My secretary, Pat Farah, answered his call. Coach asked to speak to "Buster" Turner. She responded that there was no one there by that name. He called back a second time and asked for "Buster" Turner and he received the same response as the first time. Then it dawned on Art that my real name was Paul Turner. He called back and Pat put him straight through to me. In high school I went by "Buster." From my college years on, I was Paul.

To add more irony concerning the Gamecock Club, I went to high school with the present Gamecock Club Director, Patrick McFarland's, parents, Jimmy and Connie McFarland. Connie Bradford and her family had attended College Place Methodist Church with Coach Baker and me.

After Dinner, Can We Have a Hamburger?

My wife, Jane, is not a very adventuresome eater. This goes back to the way she was raised. Her father, Eskel N. Miller Jr., was a Colonel in World War II and pretty well ran his family like the Great Santini. Whatever was cooked and placed on your plate, you were expected to eat it. This probably went back to the Great Depression when adequate food was a blessing and no food was allowed to be wasted. Jane refused to be forced to eat what she didn't like. Therefore, she was made to stay at the table until she cleaned her plate. In reality, she would stay at the table until her father took his afternoon nap. Then her mother would let her leave the table with food still on her plate. This experience made Jane have an aversion to some of her father's favorite foods, for example, tomatoes, squash, cucumbers, etc.

I recall a couple of experiences over the years when Jane was placed in somewhat of a predicament. While living in Jackson, Mississippi, a couple, Burt and Martha Curry, who were in our Sunday school class invited us to have a meal with them. Usually, when we invite people to eat with us, we cook far more food than can be eaten. In other words, we wanted every guest to eat all they wanted. After a social hour, Martha served the meal. It was four small pieces of chicken and an assortment of vegetables, most of which were not to Jane's liking. Jane's strategy/tactics in similar situations in the past was to eat more of the items that she preferred. In this case, she would normally eat more chicken. With only four small pieces of chicken this approach was impossible. She placed a very small serving of the dishes on her plate. Then after eating her piece of chicken moved the food around her plate until dinner was over. We thanked the Curry family for a nice evening. As soon as Jane got in the car, she asked, "Can we go get a hamburger?"

The second occasion, Terry and Louise Preston invited us to dinner shortly after we moved to Stone Mountain. Terry was Director of Field Services at the Centers for Disease Control. He and I had become acquainted on a trip he made to Jackson. His wife, Louise, was a gourmet cook of the first order. She had fixed an exquisite meal that I thoroughly enjoyed. I don't think Jane embraced a single dish. Again, she took very small servings and moved them around the plate. She would make the appearance on occasion of taking small bites of food. In truth, this was acting at the highest level. In fact, she had been an actress in high school. Near the end of the meal, when Terry and Louise were going to get the dessert, Jane told me, "I am looking forward to the dessert." The dessert was strawberry-rhubarb pie. It goes without saying that the dessert was not a hit with Jane. Again, as soon as we got in the car, Jane asked, "Can we go get a hamburger?"

Over the years, Jane has learned to expand the dishes that she enjoys. A good example of how far she has come is how she has embraced many Chinese dishes. When we were young, she was not keen on any Chinese food.

Acting Is Just Acting

During the time that I was an Immunization Program Consultant in the Immunization Division, I remember an incident that is funny now, but wasn't at the time. My boss and Branch Chief, Jack Kirby, when he was on leave or out of town on business, would make one of us five program consultants Acting Branch Chief. The Acting role was primarily to respond to requests by the Division Director, sign documents, and other mundane things. Close supervision of the other consultants was not a primary role. Max Pesses was made Acting Branch Chief for the day.

I went to lunch with Don Eddins, a branch chief in the Immunization Division. We often went to lunch together and sometimes discussed problems and issues. This day we were having lunch and talking over a field problem that I needed his help on. As a result, I was a little longer than usual getting back to the office. Since most days we worked well beyond normal hours, this was routine for most managers and not a problem. When I returned, Max was waiting. He must have had a stopwatch and timed my lunch hour. He got in my face and announced to everyone that I was late. Now if anyone in our branch was ever guilty of bending the rules, it was Max. Remember he was not the Branch Chief, he was the Acting Branch Chief. All of a sudden, the Irish in me came out. Max was behind my desk. I took the desk and pushed it and Max toward the window. My office was on the fourth floor. The only thing between Max and the ground was the window. In no uncertain terms, I told Max if he ever raised his voice at me ever again, where he was would be the beginning of his downfall. How about that for a pun? I never remember Max ever being anything but nice to me from then on. Acting is an acting role and was never intended to be used to discipline one of your equals, especially by one that was a chronic shirker. I am not proud of what I did, but thinking back, I would probably do it again.

Unfortunately, Max passed away a several years back and therefore cannot defend his actions. I don't think he probably could anyway.

What Chinese Restaurant?

Windell Bradford was my boss, my mentor, and my friend. Windell was Deputy Director for the Center for Prevention Services at the Centers for Disease Control and Prevention (CDC). There was no better person at CDC. He was a very good manager and he always thought everybody had worth and value. He treated everybody the same way. From the first time we met, we hit it off. This was early in my career and it lasted over decades. We normally would go to lunch together at least every two weeks. We enjoyed many eating establishments in and around CDC. One day, we decided on eating Chinese food. We both set a time and said we will see you soon.

I went to a Chinese restaurant we enjoyed and waited for Windell. Ten minutes went by and there was no Windell. My assumption was that something had come up at the last minute and he was running late. After 20 minutes went by, I became worried. I called Windell's secretary, Ann Stonecypher, now Ann Jackson, and asked where he was and had something happened. Laughing, she told me that he had just called looking for me. It seems that we should have asked at which Chinese restaurant should we meet? Windell was at one Chinese restaurant and I was at another. I am glad he was not only my boss, but my friend. We laughed about this event over the years. Ann would also laugh about it. No harm, no foul. Ann was one of the prettiest, sweetest, and nicest people I ever knew at CDC.

Where Did He Say He Was Going?

Over the years I have been known for some of the things that I say, like putting two metaphors together. An example is pandora's worms. Another is if you are not in first place, you are sucking hind wind. In simulating something quickly in my mind, sometimes unique or funny sayings come out. One day I was very busy in my office and running way behind for a doctor's appointment. As I was going out the door, I told my administrative assistant, Betty Ballinger, that I was heading to my obstetrician and would be back as soon as possible. I thought I had said that I was going to my optometrist.

Suffice is to say when I got back from my optometrist's office, I was met with smiles and giggles as I entered the building. Betty had told everybody that I was going to see my obstetrician. It was somewhat embarrassing, but funny at the same time. In the future when going to any appointment, I selected my words very carefully. In other words, sometimes what I am thinking and what I end up saying are two different things.

Friends in High Places

In about 1981, I was asked to represent the Centers for Disease Control (CDC) on a new coalition, The National Healthy Mothers and Healthy Babies Coalition (HMHB). This nonprofit coalition was formed as a result of the U.S. Surgeon General's conference on infant mortality. The mission of the HMHB was to improve the quality and reach of public and professional education related to prenatal and infant care. The lead organizations were the American College of Obstetricians and Gynecologists (ACOG), the March of Dimes (MOD), the American Academy of Pediatrics (AAP), the American Nurses Association (ANA), the National Congress of Parents and Teachers, and the United States Public Health Service (USPHS). The USPHS was why I and representatives from several other agencies were part of the Coalition. In truth the USPHS convened and administered the coalition. Over time many other organizations joined the coalition. After several meetings, additional organizations were asked to join the coalition. I remember the American Cancer Society, the La Leche League, and the Salvation Army. After the first year, a small group was elected to guide the coalition and identify and procure resources to accomplish the mission and established goals. I was selected as one of the initial steering committee members and down the road became an officer. This is a long ramble to explain the origin of what would become a very significant coalition that made a difference in childhood mortality and; of course, explain how I got involved.

HMHB was initially funded by grants from the federal Maternal and Child Health Program. By strong encouragement by some of us on the steering committee that we should not place our financial foundation totally on the federal trough, we began to obtain financial support from 501c 3 nonprofits and other institutions. With this stability, HMHB began to be a major player on the national stage. We started to have educational conferences and forums to educate politicians, policymakers, and the public about national issues and their impact on mothers and infants.

86

All this being said, at one of our major conferences we asked Betty Bumpers to be our guest speaker. Her husband, Dale Bumpers, was the former governor of Arkansas and was now a United States Senator. Betty has championed maternal and child health issues while she had been the First Lady of Arkansas. She had been close friends with Roslyn Carter when Jimmy Carter was Governor of Georgia. When Jimmy became President of the United States and launched the National Immunization Initiative, Ms. Bumpers, at Roslyn Carter's, now America's First Lady, encouragement, was one of the first states to initiate a mass immunization initiative. I was sitting at a table in the audience with other member of the HMHB steering committee and representatives from USPHS agencies, including Connie Ferraro who was representing CDC. Out of nowhere a person came to our table and whispered to me that Betty Bumpers requested that I come to the head table and sit with her. As I got up and went to the podium to sit with her, the expressions at the table where I had been seating were ones of amazement. I could see looks of what is this all about. What they didn't know was that when I was Director of the Mississippi Immunization Program, I sent staff to Arkansas to help during their Immunization Initiative. Friends of mine, Don Stenhouse and Luther DeWeese, had ridden on Betty's personal bus that toured most Arkansas counties during the initiative. I had shared drinks with her on more than one occasion. I had Betty's Metro Washington home phone number in my address book. Although I can't say I was a close friend, I can say she was a close contact. I appreciated how she genuinely cared for children and did a great deal more than talk about the issue. She made a difference. Betty Bumpers is one of my heroes.

A side story that may interest some of you. When my friend, Don Stenhouse, was retiring from CDC, I called Betty Bumpers and asked if she could get a letter of commendation for Don from the President of the United States. Bill Clinton from Arkansas was then President. She said she would do what she could do. Periodically, I would check with Don's wife Ann to see if the commendation had been received.

I was becoming to think it would not happen. Then I received a jubilant call from Don that he had received the letter. It seems that it had been there for some time, but it was at their front door which was seldomly used. When I retired several years later, Don called Betty to get a similar letter for me. However, this was during the time Bill Clinton was going through the impeachment process. I never received the letter. My assumption is that the Bumpers were staying as far away from the White House as they could get.

Even a Blind Hog Sometimes Finds an Acorn

Every year the CDC's Division of Oral Health cosponsored annually a National Oral Health Conference with the Association of State and Territorial Dental Directors (ASTDD). As deputy director of the division, I was given the responsibility to work with the state dental director where the convention would be held to find an appropriate facility for the event. The year the convention was going to be held In Tennessee, I worked with Dr. Durward Collier to select a site in Nashville. There were a number of criteria that had to be met. The facility must be near a major airport. The cost of the rooms for attendees must be reasonable. The facility must have an adequate meeting space and breakout rooms. The facility must have adequate audiovisual accommodations. The quality of food as well as food prices must be considered. I believe you get the idea. Just anyplace would not suffice. After visiting many locations throughout the Nashville metropolitan area, Dr. Collier and I agreed that the Opryland Hotel best fit our needs. Therefore, this is what we recommended to the ASTDD Executive Committee.

As a perk for choosing the Opryland Hotel, the ASTDD got a suite to use for their headquarters and to use as a hospitality room. The suite had a wet bar, comfortable sofas, chairs, tables, and a bedroom. The Division of Oral Health received a similar arrangement. The only difference was that my boss, Dr. Don Marianos, and I could not accept the bedrooms for free. We were required to pay the federal per diem for each bedroom.

When we checked in and arrived at our rooms, we found instead of a suite, our setup in fact was a penthouse. The hospitality area had large windows that looked over the cascading waters and gardens below. The windows showed clearly the main nightly performances of Lloyd Lindroth, a world-renowned harpist. It was a fantastic view every night.

We had a hospitality party the first night that was greatly enjoyed by all that attended. Everyone loved the view, the sounds, and the frivolity. In fact, they took up money and asked us to have a hospitality hour the next night. As it turned out, we had a hospitality event every night of the convention. I with the help of others would go out and buy the supplies for each night's activities.

Although this arrangement is standard operating procedure in corporate America, it is not standard operating procedure among federal managers. This special environment allowed the Division of Oral Health to connect with our state and county counterparts as never before. Therefore, the statement, "That even a blind hog sometimes finds an acorn," makes sense in this case.

A Special Hunting Trip with a Special Cousin

My first cousin, Georga Moilanen Jr., and I were close when we were growing up. His mother, Hazel, and my mother, Polly, were best friends as well as sisters. Although the Moilanen family lived in Michigan, George, Bootsie, and I spent at least two weeks with each other in the summer. This was usually a week or two for me in Michigan and a week or two for him in South Carolina. As a result, we became very close and without question were the closest cousins on the Boykin side of the family.

As adults we saw less of each other, but stayed in touch on a regular basis. George Jr. as an adult had a very successful career, eventually owning his own company that he sold for a handsome sum of money.

This is another story of its own. After all these years I don't remember what year, he invited me to come to Michigan to hunt with him and his family and friends. I accepted with no reservations.

I arrived at the Detroit airport and after securing my rifle and baggage, I was picked up by George and taken to his and his wife, Cheryl's, home in Milford. What an impressive house it was. Over the next couple of days, I rode around the area with Cheryl obtaining hunting supplies and food for our hunting trip to the Upper Peninsula (UP) of Michigan. I might add that George always goes first class. Cheryl picked up prime steaks and accessories, beverages, etc. During that time, I also obtained my Michigan hunting license.

On the day of the long trip to the UP, we loaded George's car with rifles, hunting equipment, food, and other supplies. To say loaded is an understatement. It was a pleasant drive with stops to eat, fill the vehicle with gas, and to refresh ourselves. I was really impressed with the expansive bridge that had been built across the Straits of Mackinac. The last time I had crossed the Straits of Mackinac was by ferry. I don't believe I have ever crossed a bridge that was that tall. To build such a bridge was an outstanding feat. The second thing that I saw that totally awed me was Lake Superior. It looked like we were on the shores of the ocean. I had seen and fished on other Great Lakes, but this massive Great Lake was breathtaking. The UP is very beautiful and at the same time very desolate. Even during hunting season, you see few cars. The little villages are very quaint. I remember the towns of Bruce Crossing and Trout Creek. Both were not much more than a general store and a pub. After close to 10 hours, we arrived at George's hunting lodge. Coming into the area it was sunny and balmy as a spring day. In the sky above us were two large eagles doing aerial combat above us. What a beautiful sight. My thoughts went to all the cold weather gear and sorel boots that I had bought and brought with me. In 24 hours, I would be very glad that I had brought the gear that I did.

George had inherited 40 acres and a cabin from his daddy, George Moilanen Sr. He had expanded and improved the cabin. It had a great room that was very cozy with a wood- burning stove, an assortment of chairs, sofas, a kitchen table and chairs. The lighting was from lamps that were fueled by a large propane tank. The second room was the sleeping quarters. It had numerous bunk beds with appropriate sleeping gear. That night we were joined by the rest of the hunting party. We all got to know each other, partied, and ate well.

The next day we started to scout George's property and the adjoining Wildlife Management Area. We found numerous signs and started setting up blinds in areas where each of us would hunt. As we were finishing up, it started to snow. It was a heavy snow that by sunrise the next morning was several inches deep. This November morning would be opening day of deer season. This would made finding my hunting blind interesting.

For five days we hunted. We saw deer, but no prime bucks were taken. However, I had never had any more fun. The camaraderie, the food, the social time was exquisite. After a few days most of the gang went to a nearby friend's house to use the sauna. I stayed behind and had a good bath. After a couple more days, it was time to head back to Detroit.

Since George was staying behind to winterize the lodge, he has his cousin on the Moilanen side of his family, Jerry, take me back with him to Detroit. Once we got into the lower Peninsula of Michigan around Gaylord and Grayson, we encountered a heavy snowstorm. The interstate highway was covered and many cars and a large truck had skidded off the road into the median. Jerry, who was not driving a four-wheel drive vehicle, pulled off the road and let out some air from each tire. Then we returned to the highway and headed home at 65 miles an hour. We arrived safely at George's home. The next day Cheryl took me to the airport for my return trip to Atlanta.

I will always remember this hunting trip with George. It was special in numerous ways. We always talked about doing it again with our sons, Paul III and George III, joining us, but it hadn't happened yet.

Two Grandfather Clocks Are More Than Enough

When we lived in Atlanta, we would come to our mountain home at least twice a month. Jane and I both had flex schedules and worked our required hours in four days. The fact is we both worked far more than forty hours a week, but we did it in four days. This meant I usually picked Jane up on Thursday afternoon from White Electric Company where she worked. Then we would head to our mountain home for a long weekend. We just loved the mountains. My "Mimi" Boykin was raised just outside of Asheville, North Carolina. I remember as a child that when we would go from Eau Claire to see my Big Mimi, Nellie Angel Hampton, in Woodfin, every time we would first see the mountains, she would always say, "This is God's country." That resonated with me. I knew someday, I would live in the mountains. Jane and I bought the land on Cold Mountain in 1988 and built the first part of our home in 1994. We added on a couple more times as we could afford it. We also bought more acreage over time. This is our paradise.

We had neighbors, John and Norma Simms, who lived near us. They had taken us under their wings early and we began thinking of them like a favorite uncle and aunt. They were calling for snow in the mountains and therefore we called John to find out how the weather was there. John said, "The weather is fine and come on up." Jane and I headed to Cold Mountain. As we neared the area, it was snowing very heavily. As we took Frazier Road toward our house, it was obvious that it had been snowing really hard for some time. Near our house is a steep hill. Having four-wheel drive in my Ford Explorer, I did not see this as being a real obstacle. I let Jane out at the base of the hill and near the Simms home, then I put the SUV in four-wheel drive and headed up the hill. All went well for the first 50 yards, then I started spinning with absolutely no traction. With a great deal of effort, I got the SUV turned around, picked Jane up, and headed up the John and Norma's driveway. We explained what had happened. They graciously invited us to have supper with them and spend the night. We ate supper and conversed together for some time. Then it was time for bed. They fixed a place on a pull-out sofa in their living room. We were happy, cozy, warm, and safe. God is good. After about 15 minutes, a grandfather clock boomed out the hours. This scared us half to death. Jane and I tried to go to sleep a second time. Then in 15 minutes, a second grandfather clock boomed out. This happened all night long. Suffice it to say, Jane and I got absolutely no sleep. The next morning John asked how we slept. Jane and I reluctantly told John about the grandfather clocks. John sheepishly said, "I didn't think to cut them off." The next morning the snow had stopped and it was obvious that we were not going to be able to get to our house. After breakfast, we decided to go back to Atlanta and not bother the family further. However, the snow was several inches deep and to get back to the main road, it would have to be plowed. John knew a member, Ray Chambers, of the volunteer fire department who was able to use his tractor to plow the road from their driveway down to the main road. As soon as the job was done, we gave Ray some money and thanking the Simms for their hospitality, we headed back to Stone Mountain. An interesting weekend that will always be remembered. There are angels in our midst and the Simms family filled that role for us. I don't know what the grandfather clocks would be classified as.

Always the Same Two Requests

Once we built our home in the mountains, we would leave Atlanta on most Thursday nights and drive to the Blue Ridge Mountains for a three-day weekend. We would average three weekends in the mountain home a month. One of our neighbors, John Simms, was the ring leader for a group of neighbors and their friends who went somewhere in the area for a meal on Friday night. At some point, we were included for these adventures. Many of the restaurants we visited were in Asheville. The range of cuisine and the quality of the eating establishments ranged from great to average. Usually after the meal, we would end up at someone's home for dessert and lively conversation. Jane and I entertained the group several times. They loved sitting on our front porch and looking at the mountains. We enjoyed these Friday affairs very much and developed some longtime friends. Unfortunately, many that were involved are no longer with us. As the group got older, especially John and his wife Norma, the Friday night meals altogether ceased. I can't remember the names of all those that participated at one time or another, but the nucleus was John and Norma Simms, Jim and Mary King, Cliff and Bernie Lamoreaux, Lucille Dale, Damon and Agnes Farrell, and of course, Jane and me. A few stories from these weekly events are told below.

If you happened to be in the car with John Simms, he would turn into a tour guide. He knew the history of places and landmarks. He showed us shortcuts. At the end of any trip, you knew a great deal more about Haywood County and western North Carolina than you did before. Without question John was the key to great Friday nights.

One constant was that two in our entourage, Jim King and Bernie Lamoreaux, were going to ask the same two questions at every restaurant. Jim was going to ask for root beer and Cliff was going to ask for sugar-free dessert. These questions were going to be asked even if they already knew the answer. At the Harbor Inn, one of our favorite restaurants, we usually got the same waitress. They would ask her the same two questions knowing that they didn't have root beer or sugar-free dessert. She would roll her eyes and in a kidding way scold them for asking. We would all laugh every time. Both Jim and Cliff are gone, but when I think of them, I always smile.

At another barbeque establishment, one of the waitresses that waited on us wore so much makeup that she looked like a clown. She was a good waitress and would shower you with honey, sugar child, and other words of endearment. She would always bring from our group chuckles and smiles. She made our time there very enjoyable. In addition, the food was good and abundant.

I am smiling as I write. Good friends, good food, and great conversation makes for a great night.

Forsythia Roadsidia

Shortly after building the first section of our home in the Blue Ridge Mountains, we met a special couple that live on our mountain, John and Norma Simms. They quickly became special friends that we enjoyed very much. I have already mentioned them in other stories.

Norma loved plants and flowers very much. As a result, her yard was filled with numerous plants of all kinds. Her love for gardening led her to joining a local garden club. The garden club encouraged its members to enter flower arrangements in the county fair for judging. Apparently, the garden club was very successful in receiving many first-place blue ribbons over the years. Since being in the garden club, Norma's flower arrangements had received first-place recognition more than once. One year the forsythia beside the main road, Frasier Road, going into Mount Chalet were extraordinarily beautiful. Norma made an arrangement with some of the forsythia flowers and entered it in the Haywood County Fair. She called the arrangement Forsythia Roadsidia. You guessed it. She won a blue ribbon for the best in show.

The Wrong Jane Turner

While I lived in Atlanta, I was Chair of the Atlanta March of Dimes. Since I had been Chair of the Austin, Texas, March of Dimes, I became Chair shortly after arriving in Atlanta. The two prominent methods for us raising funds were a gigantic team walk through downtown Atlanta and the Mothers March. The walk took a tremendous amount of planning and consisted of competition among businesses and organizations. In addition, it required support and entertainment for the thousands of walkers and their supporters. Walkers would get financial pledges from supporters for each mile they walked. In other words, if a team from Sears and Roebuck had a team of 10 people, the total raised would be the amount raised by each team member added together. Sears would be competing against other similar retailers like JC Penney. On the day of the event, the starting and ending point for the walk would look like a fair with game setups, free handouts, food, beverages, etc. I made the walk in three of the five years that I was chair. One year I walked with my son, Paul III, and another year with my other son, Robert. On another occasion, I organized a team of walkers from the Centers of Disease Control and Prevention (CDC). The event raised a lot of funds to prevent and treat birth defects.

The Mothers March was organized to develop block captains throughout the Atlanta metro area. Block captains would visit all their neighbors and give them an opportunity to prevent birth defects. For a couple of years, Jane Turner, Ted Turner's wife, was Chair of the Mothers March. This Jane was his wife prior to his marriage to Jane Fonda. I believe that she had been a Miss Alabama and had finished in the top five during the Miss America Pageant. A roster of March of Dimes board members and key chairs was handed out broadly. This list included also the names of spouses. Since my wife is Jane Turner. She started getting calls from people wanting Jane Turner. They wanted Ted's wife. This happened frequently and to my Jane's chagrin it was too frequently. Ironically, we had a son, Robert Turner. Ted Turner's given name is Robert. This also added to the confusion.

On one occasion, the President of the National March of Dimes (Joe Nee, I believe) scheduled a meeting with the Atlanta Executive Director, Ted's Jane, and me. He brought with him James Roosevelt, FDR's son. President Franklin Delano Roosevelt had had polio and as a result he was the founder of the March of Dimes. This was an honor for Atlanta, but there was a hidden agenda for the meeting. The real reason for the meeting was to use Ted's Jane's influence to establish a national MOD television fund-raiser on Turner's network, CNN. It never got any traction, but it was indeed a pleasure to dine with James Roosevelt.

As I write this story, I recall the many prominent people that I met and in many cases Jane and I entertained while I was involved with the March of Dimes. While in Mississippi I met: Mary Ann Mobley, a former Miss America and actress, and her husband Gary Collins, an actor; George Lindsey, most famous as Goober Pyle on *The Andy Griffin Show*; Buck Taylor, an actor best remembered for *Gun Smoke*; and Guy and Raina Hovis, a singing duo that were featured on *The Lawrence Welk Show*. In Texas I remember enjoying Slim Pickens who was a character actor and was in many John Wayne movies, and Donna Axum, a former Miss America from Arkansas. In Atlanta we entertained: Morgan Brittany, a well-known actress on *Dallas*, and her husband Jack Gill, noted movie stunt man; Jane Turner, a former Miss Alabama and Ted Turner's wife at the time, and James Roosevelt, FDR's son. Along the way I also met: Arnold Palmer, legendary professional golfer; Jane Wyman, actress and best known for being President Ronald Reagan's first wife; and Beverly Sills, opera superstar. In fact, I have pictures made with many of these famous people that are stored somewhere in the house. Maybe someday they will mean something to my grandchildren or great-grandchildren. Of all the people we met through the MOD, Buck Taylor was the most cordial and down-to-earth, Arnold Palmer was the most significant, and Raina Hovis, in my opinion, was by far the haughtiest. As a volunteer leader of the March of Dimes, I hope I was instrumental in helping prevent birth defects. It was a lot of hard work, but it did have some benefit and rewards. We eat some fantastic meals and met a number of significant people. At the end of the day, I was involved in the March of Dimes to make a difference.

Some Ungodly People in God's House

Shortly after moving to Cumming, Georgia, we joined Midway United Methodist Church. The church congregation dated back to 1838. The beautiful country church on Highway Nine seemed to beckon to us every time we passed it. Although a newer sanctuary was used for church services, the small church that had been built in the 1920s served as a lighthouse that guided us home. The old chapel had been built from the timber harvested after a tornado had destroyed the initial sanctuary. Two church members had dedicated a year of their lives building the precious church of God. The small chapel was used for special events. I remember a nativity scene and Christmas services in the magnificent structure.

Jane and I soon joined the church and a Sunday school class. As usual, I became involved in church affairs and soon started teaching Sunday school. Within the first year and half after we joined the church, the pastor, Mike Cash, was transferred and a new preacher, Charles Robinson, arrived. Although for the most part the congregation welcomed Charles, several families expected him to be exactly like Mike Cash in every way. Of course, this is an impossibility. Each preacher has their own strengthens and weaknesses. The District Superintendent (DS) of the Georgia United Methodist Church Conference knew exactly what Midway needed. They needed a visionary that could see the church moving from a neighborhood focus to a regional church. The area around the church was booming with new subdivisions going up everywhere. A fight between church factions was slowly evolving. Unfortunately, Charles Robinson was in the middle.

Charles and I liked each other from the start of his ministry. In fact, Charles asked me to be his prayer partner. We would meet for a meal routinely and pray for each other. We didn't realize at the time how important this would be. Eventually, we added another church member, Bill Stone. Over time the group who opposed Charles' appointment, became more vocal and more aggressive. They in every way were unchristian. One night at an administrative board meeting, I told them in no uncertain terms that Saint Paul would have run the lot of them out of the church by now. At a Staff Parish meeting one night when conflict along faction lines started, I told them it was good that we were meeting at night since this was when snakes surface. Bill Stone and I became Charles' Sir Lancelot. We became his protectors. Eventually we added mass to our group. I remember Greer and Judy Austin, becoming key allies. This nucleus with several others organized to protect Reverend Robinson and do what was best for the church. Our efforts included a great deal of prayer. After months, the District Superintendent (DS) called a church conference to get to the bottom of the problem once and for all. Our group met to develop our presentation before the DS. Each of us had an assigned part to present. What happened next is a God thing. After the DS called the meeting to order, he explained that local churches in the United Methodist Church are conference churches not congregational churches. The difference is very important. Pastors are assigned by the conference and not selected (elected) by the local church. In other words, the local church has input, but the DS and conference makes the decision on appointments. This set the tone for the meeting. Then he opened the meeting up to comments. Although our group was ready, we never had to say a word. Members from the congregation came in large numbers to support our preacher, Charles Robinson. This included young people who testified how much Reverend Robinson meant to them. After numerous testimonies on Charles' behalf, the disgruntled members never uttered a word. At the end of the meeting, it was very evident that Charles was on solid ground as was Midway UMC. The disgruntled members in the weeks and months ahead left the church. With this group gone our church lunged forward in a big way.

Tell me that God was not involved. Under Charles' leadership over the next several years membership more than doubled. A new state-of-the-art administration building, auditorium, and Sunday school building were also built during this time. When we moved to the mountains in 2003, the church was still gaining steam. He made a difference and he was absolutely the right man God needed to expand His kingdom.

Charles and I remain friends after all these years. We usually see each other and have a meal together when he comes to Lake Junaluska for courses or relaxation. He is now the senior pastor for the Newnan, Georgia, UMC.

People Who Made a Difference in My Professional Career

After your professional career is behind you, you reflect on the people who made a difference during your journey. Over the years you have many supervisors and you meet many people that become friends. However, there are some that impact you more than the rest. Below I will highlight several outstanding leaders that made a profound difference in my life.

The first of these people was George Dewey Bennett. As I started my public health career at the Richland County Health Department, George took me under his wing and freely imparted his wisdom and guidance. As with anyone starting their career, I had a great deal to learn and at times I felt insecure. George became my foundation and security blanket. Even though I was low man on the totem pole, at times he supported my positions when he thought I was right. He, on occasion, protected me from unreasonable demands by the state and federal infrastructure. His experience, his wisdom, and his guidance enabled me to become more proficient as a venereal disease investigator. His contacts at the state level and at Fort Jackson opened doors for me. This allowed me to expedite investigations and to obtain test results more quickly. In the process of helping me develop as an investigator, he also taught me how to be a manager. He not only became a mentor, but became a friend and in my mind the status of a favorite uncle.

My next mentor that became a lifelong friend and inspiration was Jack Benson. He was the Centers for Disease Control's' (CDC) Deputy Regional Director for the Atlanta region. During my second year in the South Carolina Venereal Disease Program, I attended my second

SC Public Health Association Annual Meeting in Myrtle Beach. At this meeting I met Jack and his wife, Betty. This very established high official treated me with respect and as if I had value. He even asked me to join them for a meal. Later, he became instrumental in me being recruited and hired to CDC's Immunization Division. When after a couple years I became CDC's Immunization Division state representative for Mississippi, Jack became my federal supervisor. He and I talked a few times every week. On site visits, he would visit my home and always wanted to see Jane and the boys. Jack was a class act and treated his employees like they had worth. He supported me fully and advocated for my program. During Hurricane Camille, he helped secure for my program the finances, vaccine, and personnel that were needed. He advocated for my promotion at a young age to become the Mississippi state representative. He advocated for my promotion as the CDC's Immunization Division's state representative in Texas. Jack was always in my corner. Once I came to CDC headquarters, Jack and his family and my family became close. As an Immunization Division program consultant, Jack's U.S. Public Health Service Region IV was one of the two regions assigned to me. As a result, Jack and I continued to work closely together and he introduced me to the staff for the eight states in his region. What Jack knew and who Jack knew was freely shared. Jack made my job easier. I could go on and on about how much I respected the knowledge and leadership of this congenial man. My career was greatly enhanced by Jack Benson. My life was enriched by his friendship. One prime example of his friendship was when he came over to our home and put up a basketball goal for my boys. He certainly had skills that I didn't possess. His reward was one of Jane's fried chicken meals with all the southern side dishes.

When I got transferred to the Mississippi Immunization Program, my new boss was Howard Boone. He was the CDC state representative and director of the program. He was a native Mississippian and had been in the state for his entire career. First, he was in the venereal disease program and then in the immunization program. He was a close friend of the Mississippi State Health Director and this probably had contributed to his long tenure in Mississippi as a senior public health advisor. Mr. Boone was older than my father and a man that deserved respect. I never was able to call him Howard. He was to me, always Mr. Boone. He was a southern gentleman in every aspect. From the beginning, he took care of Jane and me like we were his own children. The first thing he did was to secure a church friend, Ann Thomas, to help secure housing for us. We had planned to rent a home, but she found for us an FHA repossession that had been completely renovated. The small three-bedroom house fitted our needs perfectly. This was certainly instrumental in securing our financial future. I often think about the financial implications had we rented rather than purchased a home. From the beginning, Mr. Boone involved me in every aspect of the program. I learned the program from the bottom up. I helped hire staff, helped train staff, and helped supervise staff. I learned to manage the budget. After being trained by CDC, I instituted the mass measles campaign and trained staff how to develop and implement county campaigns. Within months of being assigned, I helped plan and implement a statewide immunization survey. Mr. Boone fully prepared me to run a statewide immunization program. Little did I know that he would retire 18 months into my tenure. Because of Mr. Boone and Jack Benson, I was made acting director upon Mr. Boone's retirement. I served in this capacity for 15 months. As acting director, I supervised a major relief effort along the Mississippi gulf coast after Hurricane Camille. Without Mr. Boone fast-tracking my training and management opportunities, I would never have been able to perform the way I did. I received 10 years of experience in 30 months. Howard Boone was an integral part of my development. I regret that I never really fully acknowledged all that he did for me and my family. He was a gentleman's gentleman.

Before ever coming to CDC headquarters, I met Windell Bradford at one of the annual National Immunization Conferences. Windell was very likable and never had any regal opinion about his title or worth. He treated everyone with respect and was very happy to associate with the rank and file. I think we instantly liked each other. Upon finding out that I went to church with one of his Bradford cousins, we appeared to become even more comfortable with one another. On coming to Atlanta, we continued to enjoy being together for a cocktail after work. A few months after the Immunization Division went through a reorganization, Windell asked me to take Jack Jackson's place as Deputy Chief of the Dental Disease Prevention Activity. Over the years, this activity became the Division of Oral Heath of which I became Deputy Director. Windell was always approachable and difficult problems would be resolved in his usual even and very effective management style. He was one senior manager that could be your friend as well as a supervisor. One of the Centers for Prevention's prime social activities was the annual Christmas party. Windell pushed this activity and through his leadership and promotion made it the envy of the entire Centers for Disease Control. Everyone wanted a ticket. Because of Windell's influence, Don Stenhouse, Joyce Ayers and her staff, and me, as well as others, were involved every year. In fact, we had a planning committee that functioned year-round. Windell was a mentor and a friend. In truth, he was a mentor and friend to many. After retirement, we continued to communicate regularly. He loved living in Thunderbolt, Georgia. He recently passed, but I will never forget his impact on my career and his friendship. To paraphrase the motto of the Watsonian Society, Windell is gone, but will never be forgotten.

Within a year after joining the Dental Disease Prevention Activity, my boss, Dr. Bill Bock retired. His replacement was Dr. Steve Corbin. He was dynamic and energetic. He managed the activity from Washington D.C. and left the supervision and the day-to-day operations to me. Together we started to grow the activity. With Windell Bradford, Dr. Mike Lane, and eventually Dr. Alan Hinman's support, the activity added staff and strengthened our role in the dental community. One key staff member added was Dr. Margaret Scarlett. Her hard work in infection control for the dental operatory took us into a whole new realm and moved us away from just a prime emphasis on water fluoridation. Steve was the visionary and his enthusiasm moved everything forward. We became friends and over time, even though I was five years older, he contributed greatly to the advancement of my career. Eventually, he became the Chief Dental Officer for the United States Public Health Service, with a rank of Rear Admiral. He then became Chief of Staff, for the U.S. Public Health Service Surgeon General. In the latter capacity, he and I orchestrated a plan to prevent the Division of Oral Health from being dismantled. After retirement, we worked a short while together at Oral Health America. Steve was one of the most dynamic people I have ever worked with. I am proud to call him a friend and mentor. It may be of interest that Steve married Cathy Backinger, who was another Dental Disease Prevention Activity superstar. Cathy had a stellar career with the Food and Drug Administration (FDA)

Robert Klaus is my last mentor and friend. Robert was President and CEO of Oral Health America. I first met Robert when I was still the Deputy Director for the Division of Oral Health. Oral Health America's National Spit Tobacco Education Program (NSTEP) was looking for a person to work with the Atlanta Braves and to develop and promote a community program to prevent youth from using smokeless tobacco. I became that person. I missed greatly being involved at the state and community level. This would allow me to use my public health experience and knowledge. From this meager beginning Robert and I became friends and had mutual respect for each other. Our two different worlds merged. He knew the 501 c3 nonprofit world and I knew public health and public education and promotion. We became friends and he became a mentor of mine. A couple of years later through an Inter-government Personnel Agreement (IPA), I was assigned by CDC to work for OHA. I became OHA's Director of Coalition Development and eventually became Executive Director of the National Spit Tobacco Education Program (NSTEP) working with Minor League Baseball and Major League Baseball. Upon retirement from CDC, I was hired by OHA to do a job that I would have done for free. Robert was a friend and supported my efforts. I have had few jobs that I enjoyed more. Robert exposed me to the nonprofit world. Unfortunately, the Robert Wood Johnson grant that supported NSTEP died, and thereafter, NSTEP started a steady demise and, of course, my job went with it. However, the experience that I gained, paid great dividends. I created the North Carolina Spit Tobacco Education Program (NCSTEP) and eventually received a grant from the North Carolina Health and Wellness Trust which was funded from state master tobacco settlement funds. With this grant, I was able to run the NCSTEP statewide program for seven year providing technical support to other grantees throughout North Carolina. When the NC legislature dissolved the Health and Wellness Trust, NCSTEP was by necessity reduced and then functioned on a contract basis. Robert taught me well and without question was a special friend. My life after CDC was successful because of Robert Klaus, a very special person. Unfortunately, Robert passed away a few years back with Parkinson's disease. Another very good man left this world too soon.

Is That All I Get?

Joe McGee, Don Stenhouse, and I have been hunting and fishing together for over 40 years. I will always remember the time Joe shot his first deer. In truth, he shot two deer the same morning from one of Ken Allman's stands. He had never field-dressed a deer before. The fact is that after 40 years he has still not field-dressed a deer. In his own words, he said it stinks. It must not stink to the rest of us. Over time field-dressing a deer becomes easier and the aroma more bearable. That morning another hunter, Connie Ferrara, field-dressed both of Joe's deer. Once they were back in camp, the two deer were transferred to my vehicle and carried to the processor. We had a mutual agreement between Joe and me if one of us killed two deer, we would split the cost for the processing and split the meat.

When the processor notified me that the meat was ready, I drove the 70 miles and collected the meat. I drove by Joe's house on the way home. Joe wasn't home, but Becky, Joe's wife, let me put his half of the meat in their freezer. Later, I got a call from him inquiring, "Was that all the meat I get?" Somehow, he didn't understand that after field-dressing and processing, the actual meat in packages is about 60% of the actual weight of the deer shot.

In other words, Joe's contribution was killing the two deer. The field-dressing, two trips to deer processor, and putting the packages in the freezer was done by someone else. Followed by, "Is that all I get?" By the way, over the years how Joe bagged the deer has been embellished. He shot one deer right-handed and one deer left-handed. To make the story better, we also added that the last deer was killed while he was swinging from a vine. Joe is always a good sport and laughs as we all do when we tell the story. Very few people kill two deer in the same hunt. For your first two kills to be the same morning is very rare.

Adventures on the White River

My friend, Don Stenhouse, learned about a fishing lodge, Newlands, on the White River in Lakeside, Arkansas. The trout fishing there was reported to be outstanding. After talking about it for a while, we decided to make reservations. From the first trip, we were hooked on fishing the White River. For several years, we made the annual pilgrimage to Newlands. The constant on most of the trips was Don and me. On each trip there were a different combination of characters. Some of those that joined us were: Joe McGee, our longtime hunting and fishing companion; Jeff Parker, Don's son-in-law; Garen MacDonald, Don's next- door neighbor; Rene Cote, a Stenhouse family friend, and my first cousin, Roy Neville. There were others, but I don't remember all their names. Most years, we made the very long trip by SUVs. On one trip, we flew to Memphis and took a rental car, a Ford Excursion, the last several hours to Lakeside. Over time, we always stopped in Mountain Home for groceries and other supplies. Mountain Home is less than 50 miles from Lakeside.

Newland's Lodge was a scenic establishment on the river that even had a convention center. They had comfortable cabins that could accommodate our party's needs. The cabins had an equipped kitchen, a living area with television, and several bedrooms. The front porch was covered with chairs and had a grill. The accommodations were a major step up from the environment that we had expected. One bungalow that we learned to like very much was requested every year. They offered to cook all our meals for us or they would cook specified meals. Of course, this wasn't free. Over time, we tried all they had to offer. The meals they did provide were outstanding. I remember meals with fried fish, large steaks, frog legs, potatoes and other side dishes, and, of course, dessert. There was no way we could eat everything they cooked. A meal fixed on an open fire in the outdoors beside a beautiful river was outstanding. Over time, we started to cook most of our meals ourselves with grilling out at supper being one of the major events of the day.

The reason we came to the White River was for its renowned trout fishing. At least this was true on the part of the White River where we were fishing. Where we were was close to the Bull Shoals Dam. The first part of the river closest to the dam was catch and release only. This was about a mile and half stretch. When you fish this area, you must use barbless hooks. The Arkansas Natural and Wildlife Resources rangers patrol this section to make sure that their catch and release laws are abided by. On our first trip to this area, we used guides who supplied the boat, fishing gear, and bait. Most of our successful fishing trips were with guides who were very familiar with the White River. Don and I caught a number of rainbow trout that weighed in the three, to four-pound range. These trout were gigantic compared to what we normally caught in Georgia. Don caught a brown trout that weighed about 12 pounds. What a fight Don had on his hands to land this monster. This sets the stage for many great experiences in the catch and release section of the river.

Downriver near the fish camp was outstanding trout fishing. Again, for the most part we used guides and their boats. At first, we used guides for morning and afternoon fishing trips. As we became more experienced, we learned that the morning trips produced the best fishing. At some point, we used guides in the morning and fished on our own in the afternoon. Without any doubt, this was the best trout fishing that we had ever experienced. This is true for the number of trout that we caught and the size of the trout that we caught. On almost every trip, our assorted team of fishermen would catch our limit every day. In fact, we would catch twice our limit, releasing the smaller trout that were caught. We would catch trout routinely that weighed around one and one and half pounds. These are large trout on anyone's standard. We ate trout and everybody brought fish home to eat.

As with any adventures, there are many experiences that are worth telling. The first of these stories concerned a fishing trip that included Jeff Parker, Don's son-in-law. Don had given the keys to his SUV to Jeff so that he could retrieve some fishing gear. We were fishing the catch and release area. This was one of the more isolated parts of the river and some distance from the fishing lodge. After fishing, when we got back to the car, Jeff could not find the keys to open Don's Ford Expedition. He looked everywhere to no avail. We were in somewhat of a dilemma and pondered about what we were going to do. We retraced Jeff's steps including his time in the river, in hopes of finding the keys. After some time, the ranger came by and agreed to help us. He called a locksmith and after what seemed forever, the locksmith showed up. He had no trouble unlocking the car door, but once inside the car, the locksmith found a major problem. Since Don's SUV was a new computer-generated version, the starter to the vehicle would require a Ford key that included a computer chip. In other words, a skeleton key would not start the Expedition. The only way to get a new key was to order it directly from Ford or have one mailed from Atlanta. We all were resolved to the fact that the key would have to be ordered and shipped. After making arrangements to be picked up and taken back to the cabin, we all gathered in the den of the house to plot our next steps. It was obvious that we would have to stay a few more days until the key could be ordered and shipped to Don. We were dejected and were regretting our plight. After sometime Don went to his room to stow away his fishing gear, including his fishing vests. In checking one of his vest, he found the missing keys. Somehow, when Jeff had used the keys to retrieve some gear from the SUV, once he had finished, rather than putting the keys back into his own vest, he had placed the keys in Don's spare vest. Gloom went to joy rapidly. Our problems had been resolved.

On another excursion to the catch and release section of the White River, Rene Cote was fishing with us. Rene is a purist and fishes with a fly rod. He is without question one of the best fishermen I have been around. When he starts fishing, he is very active and covers a lot of territory. In the catch and release zone you have to be aware that a loud horn can go off at any time. This means that some of the dam gates will be opening shortly and a large volume of water will be released. When this happens, the river will rise quickly. Fishermen and fisherwomen should heed the warning and get out of the river quickly. Don and I started watching Rene. He kept right on fishing. We were not sure why he wasn't getting out of the river. Did he not understand the significance of the horn blasts? We could hear and see the water rising. Rene continued to fish without any obvious concerns. Don and I were greatly concerned. Right where he was, the banks were very steep and would be difficult to climb and to compound that problem, wet waders would make it almost impossible. Shortly, he turned a bend in the river and we lost sight of him. By this time, the river had strong currents and had risen several feet. All in our party were worried about Rene. We were all thinking the worst.

Then we saw a familiar figure coming toward us on the riverbank. We were all delighted that he was safe. Don gave him a few heated words of advice. I believe Rene will get out of the river the next time the horn blasts.

Another event that included Rene Cote was him teaching me how to prepare line for my fly rod. He was doing this after several adult beverages prior to dinner, during dinner, and after dinner. He was showing me how to make loops, tie knots, etc. I watched intently and was delighted I would be ready to fish the next morning. As I am not as mechanical as some of the fishermen in our group, I was very appreciative that he had rigged my fly rod. The next morning, we all hit the river for a morning of fishing. As I began, I had trouble getting my line out using the fly casting 10 o'clock to 2 o'clock motion. No matter what I did, the line did not cooperate. According to Don, I was making so much noise splashing that everyone cleared out of the area where I was fishing. Don being the gentleman that he is, came to investigate what was going on. Once I told him about my problem and he being an experienced fly rod fisherman, he quickly detected my problem. It appears Rene did everything right, but one. He had unknowingly wrapped the line a couple of times around the rod. In this condition, I would have never gotten the line to flow smoothly from the rod. In a few minutes Don had the problem resolved and my rig operated smoothly, at least smoothly for me. I had fun fishing and even caught some nice trout. Rene had meant well, but the adult beverages had cut down on his precision.

When Jeff Parker came to the White River with us, we knew that we were in for some great meals. He is a gourmet cook and he will develop some outstanding cuisine. Stopping in Mountain Home, the closest city to Newlands, he shopped for all the groceries he would need to prepare his masterpieces. His centerpiece meal would be ribs with all the fixings. He bought two large slabs of ribs. At least he thought he had two large slabs. When the time came to prepare the ribs for cooking, there were two large slabs in each package. Therefore, he had twice as much as he expected. It took him a lot longer to prepare and cook the ribs. We ate ribs till they were coming out of our ears. They were fantastic. Everybody at Newlands were recipients of Jeff's ribs. None were wasted I assure you. Great food by Jeff makes any trip he is on better.

On one trip, Roy Neville, my cousin, accompanied Don and me to the White River. Don, as usual, drove us to Newlands in his Ford Expedition. As expected, we caught many fish and for the most part had our usual good time. There was one exception. When Don and I are not fishing, we play cribbage, sit on the front porch and watch the river, talk, read, and just enjoy relaxing. This is not Roy's style. He has to be doing something or he gets bored. When he and his brother, Johnny, and their wives would come to see Jane and me in the mountains, the same thing happens. Johnny, Barbara, Charlotte, Jane, and I can sit on the porch in our rockers and watch the beautiful mountains, and talk for hours. However, Roy wants to go somewhere and do something. On this trip, he would borrow Don's SUV to go see a golf course or go see the Bull Shoals Dam. In Tupelo where we stayed on the way home, he borrowed Don's vehicle to go see a Civil War battle site where Nathan Bedford Forrest was involved. I did accompany Roy on this trip. Don will do anything for most people, but Roy's excursions drove him crazy. Constantly borrowing his new Ford Expedition did not sit well with him. Suffice it to say, Roy did not return to Newlands with us again.

All good things eventually come to an end. As I stated earlier, we always preferred cabin (bungalow) number 5. It fit our needs perfectly and was situated where we could observe the magnificent views of the river. On this trip, Charles Newland's new wife was more involved in operating the lodge. She scheduled another group of fishermen in cabin number 5 for the last night of our stay. This caused our whole party to have to pack and move our luggage and fishing gear to another cabin for one night. This was very inconvenient and inconsiderate on her part. After all, we were regulars. Mrs. Newland's business savvy was woefully lacking. It takes Don a long time to anger, but once he is mad, look out. We never returned. We found fishing in the area around Helen, Georgia, was more convenient. Even though the fishing is not as outstanding, the fun among friends continues. Don, Joe McGee, and I have now been going there for many years.

Understanding Clearly That We Are Not Immortal

When we moved full-time to the mountain house from our Cumming house, we joined Bethel United Methodist Church. Over the years when we would come to our Cold Mountain house from Atlanta, we routinely visited this church. Therefore, we had already made some friends there. In the first year after we joined, we were invited to join a dinner club. All the members attended Bethel, with the exception of Jimmy and Janet Burke. The other members were: Rick and Kay Boen; Mike and Sue Dolata; Scott and Alicia Goodwin; Mike and Barbara McDonald; Gary and Linda Tollefson; and Rich and Sherrill Vliet. We were all about the same age with the Burkes and Goodwins being the youngest. Monthly, we would meet at a different member's home for a meal. We would have great food and wonderful Christian fellowship. From this dinner group, a Christian poker club was formed. Members of the poker club were: Gary, Mike, Rich, Rick, Scott, and me. We eventually added Scott's brother-in-law, Bill Mente. I know a Christian poker club sounds funny, but it really was a Christian poker club. We all placed five dollars in the pot at the beginning of the game and received a corresponding number of playing chips. If you ran out of chips during the game, you could buy additional chips. The big winner during the night received all the money and donated the amount to the Bethel United Methodist Church's youth program. Over time, this evolved into the winner donating the money to his charity of their choice. We had years of great fun in the dinner club and the poker club, but after several years both disbanded. As with anything in life, a number of reasons contributed to the demise. Some members started to go to Florida for the winter. Others moved away. Attendance became too irregular. Some members had a falling-out with others. I believe you get the picture.

Now the sad part that effected our group of friends. Barbara McDonald had some major health problems and passed away. A few years later Gary Tollefson, Scott Goodwin, and Mike McDonald all passed away in a two-year period of time. Without question when you lose four friends all younger than you in a very short time, you realize that you are not immortal and that life is fleeting.

Let It Ride: New Game and Big Rewards

When I was with Oral Health America, we had a staff meeting in Las Vegas. While waiting for my staff to arrive, I made a decision to go to the gaming tables. One game was called, "Let It Ride." The game sounded interesting so I sat down and let the dealer explain how the game worked. Every player is dealt two cards and everyone plays three common cards. In other words, you make your best poker hand with the five cards. You place a bet on each of three common cards and you can place another bonus bet. You are really playing the dealer not the other players. All the three common cards are dealt down and the players two cards are dealt up. As the first common card is turned over you have a choice to pull one of your bets or leave it. This is also true for the second common card. The last bet has to stay. This sounds like it is complicated, but it really isn't. After playing for a while, I felt comfortable playing "Let It Ride." Now the real story begins. After playing for about 30 minutes, I receive my two up cards that were diamonds. The first common card that was turned over was also a diamond, but since it didn't pair with either of my up cards, I pulled my bet. The next common card turned over by the dealer was also a diamond, but it didn't pair with any of my cards, so I again pulled my bet. When the dealer turned the last common card over, blinking lights went off and sirens started to whine. It scared me to death. What had happened was that I been dealt a diamond straight flush. On my $5 bet plus the $1 bonus, I had won $3000. If I hadn't pulled my other two bets, I would have won $5000. Live and learn. They shut down the table. Managers counted and checked the cards. They reviewed video footage. I guess this was to see that the dealer and I hadn't cheated. People from all over the casino congregated at the table to see what was going on. I felt somewhat conspicuous and embarrassed. After what appeared to me to be an eternity, I received a check for $3000. Then I had to sign a tax form. With my heart pounding, I gave the dealer a $200 tip. I went to the cashier, cashed my check, and placed $3000 in my bill folder. On arriving back home a few days later, I presented Jane $2800 dollars. I don't ever remember playing "Let It Ride" ever again, but the time I did play, it was exciting and rewarding.

The Best of All Our Vacations

As we get older, the good times in our past become more precious. Time seems to make some of our adventures and vacations stand out and thoughts of them may be embellished in our mind over time. In remembering the past, several vacations stand out. The following paragraphs are my attempt to highlight our most favorite vacations.

Houston, Texas, Area

When we lived in Austin, Texas, we lived in the Balcones Woods Subdivision in northwest Austin. Without question this was a very close and special neighborhood. Some of our closest neighbors were involved in our bridge club, pool activities, tennis, and other social functions. One couple, Phil and Joan Norton, and the Turners planned a trip to the Houston area. Phil being a Lieutenant Colonel at Bergstrom Air Force Base was able to obtain our accommodations and tickets for events at the military rate. This was a substantial savings that was greatly appreciated. Our families caravanned to Houston in our family cars. Since there was eight of us, one car would not have been sufficient. In Houston we spent a day at Astroworld. Another day we spent at the Astrodome, the baseball park for the Major League Baseball team, the Houston Astros. We had a great time at both facilities. Our children, Paul, Kay, Paul III, and Robert, were in hog heaven. From Houston we traveled to Galveston and spent a day at the beach. From Galveston we traveled to San Jacinto. There we visited the State Military Park remembering the great battle where Texas won their freedom from Mexico. You could feel the spirits of those who had died in the encounter. It was indeed a special place for us and a special place in Texas and American history. While in the area, we visited the USS *Texas*, one of the greatest battleships ever built. It was a tremendously large ship and we visited every part of this historical vessel. Again, you could feel the presence of those that had sailed on this great ship. I remember a meal that we had at the San Jacinto Inn. It was all you could eat crab and shrimp with all the accompanying dishes. It was a wonderful vacation and both families were completely compatible with each other. The Norton and Turner families stayed in touch for years after we both were transferred from Austin. When Phil was at the War College in Montgomery, Alabama, we stayed with the Norton family on the way to South Carolina for summer vacation. When I had business in Washington, I visited them when Phil was stationed at the Pentagon. Phil retired from the Air Force as a Colonel and Joan became a successful Realtor. Their son, Paul, graduated from the University of Texas. I am not sure what college Kay attended.

Pascagoula, Mississippi Area

After we transferred from Austin to Atlanta, we stayed in contact with our close friends, John and Dell Gully. Several months after we were settled, they called and asked us to join them on their vacation in Pascagoula, Mississippi. This is where both of them had been raised and they had abundance of family in the area. This was a no-brainer for us and we readily agreed to meet them there. We had met Dell's parents, Phil and Mildred Ware, on a few occasions and they treated us like family. When we arrived, the Ware family had arranged for the Turner household to stay on their houseboat moored on the Pascagoula River. This would be an experience for all four of us. After we got our sea legs, we were very comfortable. After a week on the boat, we had to get our land legs back. All of John and Dell's extended family treated us like we were family. We enjoyed fishing and skiing, going to the yacht club, and the fine southern cuisine that included a lot of seafood. We spent time on the river with John's brother, James, and his wife, Kay, and their daughters, Dana and Nicole. John, James, and I did a great deal of fishing in the morning and the children would ski in the afternoon. I didn't tell Jane until later that where we fished in the morning around alligators was the same water where we were skiing in the afternoon. She would not have been happy. The Gully clan had no problem skiing in the area because they had been doing it for years and years. We caught a large number of fish and netted a large amount of shrimp. Suffice it to say we had some great fish fries. James is a man that can do anything and is good at anything he does. James' children, Dana and Nicole, were about the same age as Paul III and Robert. They got along beautifully together. Paul III was smitten with the beautiful Dana. She was independent and very mature for her age. Had he lived on the gulf coast, I believed he would have loved dating her. It goes without saying more that we had a fun-filled and active vacation. The Gully and Ware families treated us like royalty and made us feel special. John and Dell have always been special to us and we have remained close over the years. We are Godparents to their son, Christopher, and since Jane kept Catherine often when she was a tot, she feels like a special niece. Dell and her family came to visit us last year and we all a wonderful time. The party included Dell, Catherine and her two children, Gabe and Ava; and Christopher and Molly, and their daughter, Quinn. Jane and I made sure that their time with us was fun and inclusive of many mountain activities. Sadly, John passed away at 54 from cancer. A very sad day for Jane and me. John was the best Christian man I have ever known.

Detroit, Michigan Area

When the boys were somewhere around 12 and 16, we went to visit my Aunt Hazel and my cousin, George Moilanen (Bootsie), and his family in Detroit, Michigan. Aunt Hazel was my mother's closest sibling. Growing up, our families visited each other almost every summer. Bootsie, now George, and I would stay a week or more together most summers either in Detroit or Columbia. During a couple summers we spent a week in both places. George is still my closest cousin on the Boykin side of the family. The Moilanen family always goes out of their way to give visitors, especially family, a special time. We did all the tourist things. One of the highlights was visiting Greenfield Village. This amazing village features a great deal of history with some of the most prominent figures being Henry Ford, Thomas Edison, and Harvey Firestone. Of course, many other significant contributors to our great American history were included in the museum. I believe you could stay there for days and not absorb everything. We also visited Windsor, Ontario, Canada, for a day. We visited a water park. George took us to the golf club where he was a member for an afternoon of activities and a meal. This list goes on and on. We had a full agenda each and every day. Aunt Hazel's philosophy was that if you are not worn out at the end of your vacation, it was not a very good vacation. We enjoyed many very good meals during the trip. George and Cheryl's two children, George III and Gwen, were about the same age as Paul III and Robert. The four bonded as cousins during the trip. Paul III and George III have continued to communicate with each other over the years. One humorous event happened toward the end of the trip. At least it is humorous now, but it wasn't at the time. The four young people went to an amusement park by themselves. According to Aunt Hazel's assessment, it was not very far. You must know that this was Aunt Hazel's measurement for most trips we went on. She would say, "It is not far." An hour and a half or two hours later we would arrive. The four young people headed to the amusement park with George III driving. After dark, Jane and I were expecting the young people to be home. After hours of pacing and waiting, the gang returned way after midnight. It seems that not far was Ohio, more than a few hours away. If we had known this, our expectations for their arrival home would have been greatly adjusted. Jane and my controls on our boys were a great deal tighter. All that ends well is good. Paul III and Robert had had a great time. The trip to Detroit had been special. Being with family was even more special.

Europe: Germany, France, Luxembourg

A trip to Germany to see one of Jane's closest friends, Beryl Newsome, and her new husband, Andy, was without question one of our greatest trips. Beryl had been in Germany for many years. After she was divorced from her first husband, Jon Snelling, she had remained in Germany. Andy was career Air Force and stationed at Ramstein Air Force Base. Beryl encouraged us to come for a visit before they transferred back stateside. From the time Andy picked us up in Frankfurt, the vacation of many exciting sites and adventures started. Frankfurt is a large and bustling cosmopolitan city. This was our first exposure to Europe and we relished all the beauty and sounds. We had a significant drive to Kaiserslautern. Jane and I loved seeing the countryside and the quaint homes and homesteads. Once on the base we arrived at Beryl and Andy's substantial condominium. Rank has its privileges. It was good to see Beryl and enjoy her bubbly personality. I should add that because I had a large number of Delta frequent miles, we were able to fly first class to Germany. This was also true on our second trip to Europe. Jane thinks this is how everybody flies. The truth is if we ever cross the pond again, she will expect the same treatment. I can tell you flying first class makes long flights a great deal easier.

Starting the next day our adventures began. We toured the base and Kaiserslautern. This included enjoying some of the local cuisine. Andy took me to pub on base where I met some of the officers and noncommissioned officers with whom he worked. The following day, Beryl took us on a day trip to Wuppertal, Trier, and Luxembourg. Part of the trip was on the autobahn and it is some experience to have cars passing you at over 100 miles per hour. Wuppertal was a beautiful German village with some of the homes dating back hundreds of years. The first floor of these houses was actually the second floor. They were built during the Middle Ages where the ladder to the first floor (really second floor) could be retrieved when they were under attack. This was a defensive mechanism. I remember the beautiful antique opera house in the middle of town. The suspension railroad that had built in the early 1900s was one of the main highlights. Jane's father, Eck Miller, had been a battalion commander under General George Patton during World War II. His artillery disabled the railroad during an attack on the town. Colonel Miller respected the German people, certainly not the Nazis, so much that he had his engineers repair the railroad before his battalion departed the area. Because Beryl spoke fluent German, she purchased tickets so that we could ride the train. What a treat that was. To remember Wuppertal, we bought a souvenir bus to give to her daddy. The next town we visited was Trier, another ancient village. We were intrigued by the large gate that had been built by the Romans. It was substantial and very sturdy. We also bought some Swarovski crystal while we were there and had it shipped back home. Our next leg of the trip was to Luxembourg. Another country with magnificent homes and interesting architecture. The highlight was the American Cemetery with the graves of literally thousands of American soldiers who had given their lives to keep us free. Their spirits could be felt as we walked the cemetery. We also saw General Patton's memorial and grave. He had wanted to be buried with his troops. With this full day completed, we headed home.

Andy helped us secure some bus trips at the military rate to Paris, France, Bavaria, and Black Forest. Our first trip was to Paris. After a significant bus ride, we arrived in Paris. The ride was not a waste as we enjoyed the scenery along the way. How exciting it was to be overseas. Paris is a beautiful city, but not the cleanest city we had ever seen. The Parisians, not the French, are haughty and not very friendly. For the most part they refused to speak English even though they could. They appeared to like our money, but not Americans. We experienced France as best we could in two days. We saw the Arc de Triomphe coming into Paris. I went up into the Eiffel Tower. Jane liked seeing the Eiffel Tower, but wanted no part of seeing it closer.

We spent a half day in the Louvre. Of course, this was exciting. In order to see it in more detail, it would have taken a lot longer than the time we were allowed. The two items I enjoyed most was seeing the Mona Lisa and a smaller version of the Statue of David. We never realized how small the Mona Lisa was. The visit to Notre Dame was half full-filling. We saw the cathedral up close, but because a worship service was in progress, we were not allowed to enter. The recent fire now makes the fact that we didn't see the inside of Notre Dame even more disappointing. We were unable to see the Paris Church of the Holy Sepulchre closely because of road construction. A night cruise on the Seine was breathtaking, especially seeing Notre Dame from the river. We were able to see the regal Versailles. The beautiful structure is filled with history. The grounds are superb. The amount of gold and mirrors in the palace is unbelievable. Intermingle the marvelous French cuisine that we were able to enjoy while we were there, this short trip was outstanding in every way

We got back to Ramstein Air Force Base and decompressed and visited Kaiserslautern and again enjoyed some wonderful local meals. Then we were off on another bus trip. This time, we were off on a trip to both Bavaria and the Black Forest. The beauty in these parts of Germany is exquisite. I was particularly impressed with the much older homes where they kept the farm animals on the first floor (basement) and the living quarters were on the above floors. This certainly was the living style hundreds of years ago. We visited several castles that were built in the Middle Ages. They were substantial fortresses, but for the most part the living quarters were spartan even for the nobility. You may think that once you have seen one old castle, you have seen them all. This was not true for the regal castles that we visited: Neuschwanstein Castle and Schloss Linderhof. Without question the most magnificent castle was King Ludwig I Neuschwanstein. The outside was breathtaking. It was the model for the centerpiece for Disney World. The interior looked like we were back at Versailles. Gold and mirrors were used lavishly throughout the structure. The furniture, tables, draperies, and accompaniments were unbelievable. Another highlight on this trip was our visit to Oberammergau. This quaint village homes were colorfully decorated with murals on their sides. The town is the site of the world-renowned Passion Play which is conducted every ten years. Our bus driver knew the Pope's carver, Hans Zundert, at least I think that is the way his name was spelled. We got to meet him. He had been in every Passion Play since he was six years old. In order to be in the Passion play, you have to be a Christian and have unquestioned high morals. We bought a rock eagle from him that we still treasure. Of course, we continued to enjoy wonderful German meals during our travels.

The last part of our visit was a very enjoyable trip to another part of Germany. Having Beryl and Andy join us and guide us made for a wonderful trip. The first place we visited was the Technik Museum in Sinsheim. I have been to the Smithsonian several times and I am always awed by what I see. At the Technik Museum, I was completely blown away. If you wanted to see any year and model of a car, they had it. If you wanted to see any uniform, any weapon, any armament from World War II, they had it. It appeared that they had any and everything from the past. Visiting one large building after another, Jane and I could not believe what we were seeing. We enjoyed our time there, but did not come close to seeing everything. It was a marvelous experience. One of our night's lodgings that was arranged by Beryl was in an old castle. I remember a small chapel, and the taxidermy of a large brown bear and large boar at the entrance to where we ate supper. The meal was wild game that still today makes me salivate. The experiences, the scenery that we saw, and the history we encountered on this trip will always be remembered.

The visit to see Beryl and Andy while they were in Germany was special in numerous ways. We had never been anywhere and done so much in such a short period of time. Their friendship and hospitality will always be special. We are still close today. Andy, Beryl's son, Brad, Paul III, and I hunt together almost yearly. Our first trip to Europe was outstanding and this was largely because of our friends, the Newsomes.

England

Our next overseas trip was to England. Since our ancestry goes back to Great Britain, it was exciting to now be where some of our forefathers and foremothers had walked. England is a beautiful country and you can stay busy in London without traveling anywhere else. However, we traveled to many parts of the country. While in London we used the Tube regularly and used day passes on double-decker buses. From our hotel, we could get easily to anywhere in London. Near our hotel, the Tavistock Square Hotel, we could purchase day bus trips to every part of England. After we checked into the hotel, we rested for a little while and then decided to go to the British Museum which was nearby. It is much like our Smithsonian Museum. It has relics and displays from all over the world. I believe you could stay there for days without seeing everything. At the end of our visit, Jane and I concluded that we didn't need to go anywhere else in the world because the English had brought the world to London. On another day we came back to the British Museum for a second visit. In London we visited art museums, Buckingham Palace where we saw the changing of the guard, Trafalgar Square, Churchill's War Room (bunker), Parliament, Big Ben, Westminster Abby, Saint Paul's Cathedral, The Tower of London, London Bridge, and the list goes on and on. The Tower of London was one my favorites. I particularly liked King Henry VIII's warhorse with armor and his personal battle armor. Jane and I enjoyed seeing the Crown Jewels. I was amazed at the hundreds of original military Enfield Rifles that filled rooms. On our anniversary, we went to have a meal and to see the *The Buddy Holly Story* in Leicester Square. Jane's boss, Gary Clodfelder, had recommended the show and had given her the money to buy the tickets. It was a fantastic show and well worth attending. A couple of side stories demonstrate how there are differences when you eat out. At the restaurant in Leicester Square where we went for our anniversary meal, I asked for more bread. We got it, but found it was an extra charge. At a pizza parlor, I asked for a refill of coffee. The waitress laughed and said, "You must think you are in America." There is no such thing as refills in England. A second anything cost the same as the initial order.

We took several bus trips to sites in England. We went to Leeds Castle and visited one of King Henry's estates. It was magnificent. On another trip we went to Windsor Castle and enjoyed seeing the castle and the nearby town. The shrines to Prince Albert knights of the past, and seeing where royalty had lived for centuries and in some cases had been married, was a significant experience. On another day trip we went to Dover and saw the Cliffs of Dover, the sea, and the underwater route to France. A special experience was going to Canterbury Cathedral. It was much to take in, but the fact that it was built in 1000 AD by William the Conqueror was astonishing. The number of crypts in the basement of the church were massive. Many that were laid to rest there were the rich and the famous from history. The statue of the Black Prince was a work of art. One personal note, the Turner genealogy states that the Turner family had come over with William the Conqueror and were nobility. To Jane and my amazement, a very large plaque in Latin was a memorial to Sir Ian Turner. The plaque was erected in the early 1000s. This to me confirmed my history. On another bus trip we went to Stonehenge and the surrounding villages. Stonehenge is truly one of the wonders of the world. Mystery surrounding this creation and the meaning of the structure is very apparent as you roam around these tremendous stones. The thatched roofs on some homes in the area are a marvel and have been maintained over the centuries.

The trip to England was a wonderful experience. The English love Americans and we love the English. At least, we have been come very close since World I and World War II. Our mutual history truly bonds us. The country is not only historic, but it is very beautiful country.

English history goes back thousands of years and is unparalleled in America. Jane and I would give our trip a strong A rating. The one weakness we saw during the trip was that the English cuisine is not anywhere near the extraordinary German and French cuisine that we enjoyed on our first trip to Europe. We learned quickly that the best food was in the English pubs.

California Here We Come

Jane and I went on a Road Scholar trip with my cousin, Roy Neville, and his wife, Charlotte, to California. The Road Scholar trip started in Sacramento and included trips to Reno, Carson City, and Virginia City. However, prior to arriving in Sacramento, we took a rental car to Oakhurst, California, for a few days to visit Yosemite National Park.

The visit to Yosemite was fabulous, but because of bad weather, particularly heavy fog, it took us two days to see the numerous views and sights. The first day, we hired a guide to take us around the park. As stated earlier, heavy fog prevented us from seeing the many sights or at a minimum prevented us from seeing them well. Because Roy and Charlotte had visited Yosemite before, we took our rental car and returned the next day. What a contrast, the day was sunny, warm, and delightful. I was very impressed with El Capitan, Half Dome, and Sentinel Dome. Of course, Yosemite Valley itself was magnificent. We watched as people climbed the straight-up sheer sides of El Capitan. It was amazing to see climbers resting hundreds of feet above the ground on the sides of the cliffs in what looked like sleeping bags. I remember thinking no way would I have ever done that. I was also amazed that anyone would want to risk their lives doing that. After seeing Yosemite National Park, I clearly understand why the world-famous photographer, Ansel Adams, would use this park for his base of operation. Many of his breathtaking and fabulous pictures were taken there. Seeing is believing. Yosemite National Park is one of our greatest National Parks.

After seeing Yosemite National Park and spending one more night in Oakhurst, we headed to Sacramento for our Road Scholar trip. I remember the last night in the motel, we watched the South Carolina versus Louisiana State football game. It was a great game with the Gamecocks losing in a very close game. It would be one of our only two loses in an 11 win, two lose season.

Sacramento is a great city with much history. I remember the California State Railroad Museum which featured many locomotives from the past. There were many railroad cars. This included cabooses and some stately old Pullman cars. It was amazing to touch and see history right before you. To see the Monument where the Pony Express ended (or started depending on your perspective) during the Pony Express's short run brought back mental shots of riders being chased by Indians and galloping through the wide-open prairies. The old town part of Sacramento with many historical buildings was a vivid reminder of the city's past. Of course, the California state capital was well worth the price of the tour. We had a very enjoyable meal one night on a boat in the Sacramento River. I could go on and on, but I believe you get the picture. Sacramento is now a very large modern city with a great deal to see and do.

From Sacramento the Road Scholar tour went to Reno by train through the Sierra Nevada Mountains. What fantastic scenery we saw along the way. The mountains were rugged, beautiful, and breathtaking all at the same time. I would have to say that the train trip was one of the main highlights of the whole tour. After a few hours on the train, we arrived in Reno, Nevada.

In Reno, we stayed at a local casino and hotel. Of course, many of us took advantage of the gaming opportunity and partook of the restaurants on the property. I believe my cousin, Roy, and his wife, Charlotte, enjoyed the gaming more than anybody else on the trip. On the other hand, my wife, Jane, liked gambling the least. From Reno we visited by bus to Donner Pass where a wagon train of settlers heading west was snowed in with many succumbing to the elements. Some of the settlers survived by reverting to cannibalism. The Donner Monument and the Museum at the Donner Pass were impressive. On our trip to Donner Pass, we visited Lake Tahoe and had a meal on the famous lake. The area is very beautiful and the lake is one of the deepest in the world. We also visited an old casino and resort during this trip that was frequented by many famous people from Hollywood. I remember that Frank Sinatra performed there, among other famous performers from the past. From Reno we also made trips to Carson City, Nevada, and visited Nevada's state capital and the surrounding neighborhood. Carson City is certainly not your normal capital city. It is a quaint town and the capital itself is very modest compared to other capitols that I have seen around the country. We also visited Virginia City, Nevada, an old gold mining town, that looks a great deal like it did when mining was full bore. An old school house that had been turned into a museum was full of interesting relics from the past.

After the Reno area experience, we boarded the train for our return trip to Sacramento. Being tired, the return train trip was not as enjoyable, but the scenery was just as amazing. After our last night in Sacramento and a good meal with the group on our tour, we flew back home.

Jane and I enjoyed traveling with Roy and Charlotte and reflect back to what a wonderful time we had on the trip. A side benefit of the trip, we met a wonderful couple, Bruce Setter and Francis Ripley, from Jacksonville, Florida. We enjoyed each other so much that we went on a Road Scholar trip to Philadelphia together later. One additional benefit, Richard, "Buddy", Robinson and his wife, Deborah, who lived in Carson City met us in Reno and treated us to a very nice meal. Buddy and I went to school together from elementary school through high school. We also attended the University of South

Carolina together for three years. We played football together on a great Eau Claire High School team. Unfortunately, Buddy passed away a few years later.

Destin

For several years our son, Paul III, and his wife, Kathy, rented a marvelous three-story home in Destin, Florida. The house had room for the whole family and included a pool, an elevator, and a pool table. You could see the ocean from the second-and third-floor porches. It was wonderful that most of the family was able to participate for the whole week. The togetherness made the week special. The first year, we ate the main meal of the day at some of the best restaurants in Destin. The food was exquisite and abundant. Most facilities had magnificent views of the ocean or harbor. After the first year, we had some of the main meals at the house, but ventured out too. We always cooked a good breakfast and Paul III and Kathy had a substantial lunch, usually around the pool. The swimming pool was the centerpiece for most family get-togethers. The pool table always resulted in some lively competition. Paul III's years of practicing and playing pool in our basement in Stone Mountain resulted in him being the best of the best. The week consisted of many planned activities in the area. Trips to the beach which was just across the street from our quarters was a daily occurrence unless the weather was bad. Trips to go bowling, to visit amusement parks, and shopping were routine. The main highlight of the week was the yearly deep-sea fishing trip. Deep sea in this case was about 40 miles out in the Gulf of Mexico. We would first catch our bait fish in the harbor and then we would ride a couple hours to the main fishing areas. Paul III always contracted with Captain Brady Bowman and the boat, Bow'd Up. We always caught numerous fish. I remember red snapper, amberjack, grouper, target, several sharks, and many other varieties. When we arrived back to the harbor, without fail we would have caught more and larger fish than any other boat. Spectators in large numbers gathered to see our catch displayed on the dock. At the end of the 12-hour day, we were exhausted, but very happy and content. Toward the end of the week, Paul III and Kathy always set up a family picture-taking session at some amazing venue, like on the ocean, at a state park, or at some beautiful setting on the island. The vacations were always a great deal of fun. However, the main highlight of the week was being together as a family. Jane and I will always be indebted to Paul III and Kathy for keeping the family close and including us in these endeavors.

As I review this story, I reflect that we didn't vacation in Destin in 2020 because of the COVID-19 pandemic. However, Paul III and Kathy have reserved another house for this year in July. This house has a pool, fronts a lake, and has a view of the ocean. We are looking forward to another family outing on the ocean.

Alaska Cruise

Jane and I were able to go on a couple of Carnival Cruises with some of our Eau Claire High School schoolmates. Although we enjoyed these cruises, our trip to Alaska on the new Norwegian ship, *Joy*, took the whole meaning of a cruise to another level. The ship, the service, the food, and the onboard amenities were superb. The gourmet dining of French, Italian, and American steak house cuisines was outstanding. In other words, sailing Norwegian was in a class by itself or at least it was when compared to Carnival. Our cruise started in Seattle, Washington. It is a city worth seeing and visiting. The Alaska trip included ports in Ketchikan, Juneau, Skagway, and Victory, British Columbia. Each port included a lot to do and see. To enhance our journeys, we booked excursions in advance. Each excursion was exciting and spiritually rewarding. The first old Russian settlement that we visited was Ketchikan. It was a quaint town with stores and restaurants in abundance near the port. Jane and I went on a boat trip to see the wildlife and the Federal wildlife management lands. It was an enjoyable trip and we saw lots of birds. We especially enjoyed the majestic eagles. The vegetation and trees were different from anything that we had ever seen before. The fauna in the area was very scarce on that day. We expected to see bears, mountain goats, etc. We did get to see a few porpoises. One site that we saw looked like a small island with a cluster of evergreen trees. It was actually the peak of a dormant volcano that was underwater. This excursion was the least rewarding of the four we took, but still rewarding because it was our first encounter with Alaska. The next port was Juneau and being the capital more significant. We saw the Alaska state capital and where their legislative body convened. I thought it was very interesting that most representatives had to get there by boat or plane. A road system as we know it in the states is very limited in Alaska. Juneau was a thriving place. The homes were built very sturdy to endure the harsh winters. Our excursion took us to see the whales. We saw numerous humpback whales and at times they were all around us. We saw a rare sight according to our guide. We saw a whale actually breach. It looked like the Pacific Life commercial. It came entirely out of the water and then made a very significant splash. I would have loved to have had a video running at the time. The next port that we visited was Skagway. We liked this Russian settlement best. It was in my opinion more scenic and more authentic to my mental image of a Russian settlement. The excursion by train from Skagway to White Horse, Canada, and back was breathtaking. This was the same trail that many gold miners used to get to the Alaska gold fields. That is, the miners that didn't get there by ship. The views were outstanding. The steep grades and the ruggedness of the terrain created in us an amazement at what the old gold miners were willing to endure to pan for gold. There was no wonder in our minds why so many lost their lives in the attempt. Our cruise from Skagway to Victoria was filled with scenic beauty that one only dreams about. The glaciers, vegetation, waterfalls, and floating ice blocks the size of islands intermingled with porpoise and orca whales were spectacular. At Victoria, British Columbia, Canada, we took another excursion that took us through this beautiful modern city with many beautiful old castles, hotels, auditoriums, and buildings. A few of the plethora of wonderful structures that I remember were: Castle Victoria; Hatley Castle, and the Empress Hotel. The highlight of this trek without question was Butchart Gardens. The gardens were significant because of the sheer number of blooming and beautiful flowers, the abundance of plants, the springs, the waterfalls, and the fountains, but most of all it was the layout and the presentation. Butchart Gardens were the most amazing gardens that Jane and I had ever seen.

After another day at sea, we arrived back at Seattle. We were tired and ready to be back in the mountains. We had had a wonderful experience that will always be remembered. The Alaska cruise will be very hard to top. If we plan another cruise, it will definitely be with Norwegian Cruise Lines.

Don't Fear Vaccine, Revere Them

Jane and I, after having to wait a couple weeks after registering, received our first shot of the Moderna COVID-19 vaccine. After a month, we received our second dose. We now should both be protected from the coronavirus. I don't remember ever wanting a vaccine as much as I did this immunization. Being older and at greater risk from COVID-19, it just makes sense to be immunized. It is amazing how some people, particularly those in the antivaccination group, state that they and their family will not be immunized. It appears they fear the vaccine more than the disease. This totally does not make sense to me. With a raging pandemic all around us, why in the world wouldn't you want to protected yourself and your family from a killer virus. At this point, more than 500,000 people have been killed by COVID-19 and certainly more will die in the future. The new vaccines have been proven very safe and are more than 94% effective. In other words, at least 94 out of 100 people immunized with two doses will have total protection. As a former Centers for Disease Control program consultant in the Division of Immunization, this is the most reliable vaccine that I ever remember. Current research shows that these vaccines have minimal side effects. You could administer sterile water and a small number of people would have some kind of reaction. Jane and I both tolerated the vaccine very well. We did have a sore arm for a couple days with the first dose. We had no aftereffects from the second dose. I have no problem with people not taking the immunization. That is their right. However, I do resent it when they purposely scare others with unfounded claims and cause them to question the value of the vaccine. I also resent them placing themselves at risk and then potentially acquiring the infection and spreading it to others. This is a disservice to public health and the community.

As a former Director of the Mississippi Immunization Program and the Federal manager for the Texas swine flu program, I know vaccines work. In Mississippi hundreds of thousands of children were immunized for measles and as a result morbidity and mortality from the disease were greatly reduced. Later, young people were immunized in large numbers with rubella vaccine and the number of cases dropped drastically. The number of children born with major birth defects because their mothers had had rubella during the first trimester of pregnancy also dropped drastically. Vaccines reduced cases of diphtheria, pertussis (whooping cough), and tetanus. Polio and smallpox that use to be a worldwide problem with devasting impact on populations have been eliminated because of an effective vaccine. Without immunization we would still be seeing large numbers of communicable and debilitating diseases and unnecessary deaths. When you hear people preaching against vaccines and telling you how bad they are, remember how they have protected the world and how they have improved our quality of life. Yes, there might be a few severe-reactions in some people, but for the most part vaccines are very safe and effective. Do not fear vaccines, but revere them.

Make a Difference

As my professional career was winding down, I accepted an appointment by the Haywood County Board of Commissioners to the Board of Health. My decision to serve was easy. My whole adult life had been spent making a difference in people's lives. That is why I joined the U.S. Public Health Service out of the University of South Carolina. That is why I became a Jaycee. That is why I became involved in the March of Dimes. This was true when I became associated with Oral Health America. It was a constant when I joined churches everywhere Jane and I lived. When I joined a church, I became involved in the administration of the church at some level, including teaching Sunday school. Certainly, I benefited from my various involvements, but the driving force behind my associations was to make a difference in the community, the state, and the country. Therefore, it was natural for me to become a board member on the Haywood County Board of Health. I felt my long career in public health and my management and policy-making experience would be valuable to the county. The first year was a learning experience, but at times I was able to contribute to policy and management decisions. My contributions must have had value to the Board of Health because the next year I was elected Chair of the Board of Health. During the following year a study was conducted with the Board of Health being heavily involved to consolidate the Board of Health and the Board of Social Services into one consolidated agency. The consensus was that such a decision would be a good move and that a lot of duplication, especially from an administration standpoint, would result. In the long term, services would be improved and more economical. Of course, there would be some anxiety and some functions at the management level would have to change. After the study, the Haywood County Board of Commissioners voted to consolidated the two agencies into the Haywood County Health and Human Service Agency (HHSA). With the new agency established, the two boards would be consolidated into one. At the first combined HHSA Agency Board meeting, I was elected the first Chair. Now the work started to make the transition period as easy as possible, to keep morale high, and make the new agency effective.

As I write this story, I have been the Chair of the Haywood County

Health and Human Services for seven years. The Board has elected me annually to be their Chair. During my term we have improved the agency funding and staffing. The Board has become more proactive and deeply cares about the Agency's mission. We keep our commissioners and the community educated on issues, staffing needs, budget needs, and potential community problems. Our primary job is to advise the commissioners. The Board has evolved into members with great backgrounds that are interested and involved in the community. No longer a rubber-stamp board, but an involved board that works closely with agency management to make a difference in the community. My vision for the agency is to be fully funded and fully staffed and to have a maximum health and human services impact on our population, especially children. I continue to work closely with the HHS Agency Director, Ira Dove, and his Division Directors as well as the County Manager, Bryant Morehead. Recently, Ira, Bryant, and I worked together to screen candidates for the position of Public Health Director. This helped Ira find and select the best candidate. Together we continue to work to improve staffing and salaries and benefits for our employees. We are working to better serve the community. The current COVID-19 pandemic has been a challenge for our agency and for the county. We are currently working on one of my pet projects educating county leadership and the community about preventing adverse childhood experience (ACEs) and the trauma that results. I could go on and on, but this is my way of demonstrating that as Chair of the Health and Human Agency Board, I have had heavy involvement in the county at many levels. My hope is that I have made a difference. My service has been rewarding and I have learned to deeply care even more about those in our county that need help and protection, especially our children.

SECTION **2**

Children

Jane and I enjoyed both of our sons, Paul III and Robert, as they grew from children to men. This section tells some of the many stories that concern them.

A. Paul III
A Major Disappointment Without Any Understanding

During the summer when Paul III was a little over five years old, my grandfather, Robert Herman Boykin, took us fishing to a friend's pond. This was exciting on two fronts. First, this was Paul III's first fishing trip. Second, Granddaddy was one of the people who taught me to love fishing. Granddaddy Boykin took charge of the trip and took him under his wing. He taught Paul III how to put the worm on the hook. He taught him how to cast. When he would start talking, Granddaddy would explain how you must be quiet to catch bream. When Paul III would become fidgety, Granddaddy would explain how you must have patience to fish. This was exciting for me as well as for my young son, because this was the exact training that he had given me years ago when I was very young. After a while, Paul III caught his first fish. It was not a very big one, but his excitement was through the roof. Now his attention was on catching another bream. A little later, he caught another and then another. How much fun the three of us were having. We kept the larger bream and later cleaned them to eat. What a great time Pop Boykin had with his grandson and great-grandson. Paul III was in heaven and already asking about his next fishing trip. Pop said the next time we came from Mississippi to Columbia, we would go fishing again. Paul III wanted that to come sooner rather than later.

Now for the sad part of the story, several weeks later Pop died of a cerebral hemorrhage. The next trip to Columbia was for his funeral. Paul III expected to go fishing again with Pop. When I told him that we would not be going fishing, he said, "Pop said we would go fishing on our next trip." How do you explain to a five-year-old that he had his last fishing trip with his great-grandfather? The only consolation to this whole affair is that Paul III would always remember catching his first fish with Pop Boykin.

Rowdy Group Tamed

When we were in Austin, Texas, our son., Paul III, was in the Boy Scouts. I was one of the troop's adult leaders. I did this for two reasons. One reason was it allowed me to be close to Paul III. The other reason was that I have always liked the outdoors and camping. The Boy Scouts gave me an opportunity to do both. The Boy Scouts are allowed to go places, to see things, and do things that very few people have an opportunity to do. I remember we went on one trip to a special place near Lampasas and allowed to dig for arrowheads, spearheads, Indian pottery, etc. Paul III and his friends found numerous artifacts and were allowed to take them home. The owner did not allow the general public on his property.

On another trip, we went to the Aransas Wildlife Refuge near Aransas Pass, Texas. This was a magnificent refuge with a wide array of birds and animals. Some of the birds were rarely seen anywhere else and a few were endangered species. Peccary, a pig looking mammal, were everywhere. The first night we set up our camp before heading out the next day on our adventures. The scouts were very excited and ready to go. Having been cooped up in the vehicles for hours added to their friskiness. A few had become downright rowdy. We erected our tents, built a campfire, and fixed supper. As it became dark, we all gathered around the campfire for some camaraderie and story-telling. When it became my turn, I told the story about the devil and the Bermuda Triangle. I made up the story up as I went. After all these years, I only remember the main theme of the story. The devil was real and always nearby and that at the Bermuda Triangle which is in the middle of the ocean, many a ship and many a sailor had been taken and destroyed by the devil. Since we were on the ocean, the Bermuda Triangle and the devil to these boys were nearby. I told the story in a very eerie style. The rowdy boys that had been frolicking everywhere, remained near the campfire until bedtime. My story had calmed the rowdy group. The boys, according to Paul III, never left the tent the whole night, not even to relieve themselves. The devil was nearby and ready to feast on young boys.

The Tires Stopped, but the Car Kept Going

Paul III had several cars that he used when he was growing up. He owned two of the cars that he drove. The car that he drove right after he got his driver's license was my 1968 Plymouth Valiant. I bought this car from my Mimi Boykin after my Pop Boykin had died. The car gave good gas mileage and the slant-6 engine was mechanically sound. The engine was actually an airplane engine cut in half. I just had the car repainted about the time he started to drive. Jane and I enjoyed driving the Valiant and we had no problem with the way it looked. Paul III on the other hand did. Although he didn't like the car's looks, he still used it frequently, including when he dated. However, when it came to major events, he used his mother's Buick LeSabre, which he wrecked once. Thinking back, I believe he wrecked the Valiant once too. I do remember that when he put gas in the Valiant, he resented me using any of the gas. A lesson on what he was getting free, such as insurance, oil changes, repairs, etc., would become evident in the next story.

My boss, Jack Kirby, gave Paul III his mother's Buick Skylark. I can't remember the reason Jack got the car, but he gave it to Paul III. It was a step up in looks and horsepower. How elated he was with the gift. In receiving the car, we had a mutual understanding, it would be his car and therefore in his name. He would be responsible for the insurance, oil changes, tires, repairs, etc. He readily agreed to these terms. In order to meet this obligation, he found a job at the Hungry Fisherman. His job was as a general flunky that did everything. He had long night hours while still attending high school, including playing football. He has never been scared of hard work. With some of his first money, he had the Skylark painted and then got some high-end tires. The car looked sharp and he was very proud of the transformation. He was in hog heaven. Several months later after shouldering the financial load on his new car, he had an epiphany. He told me one day that he now knew how good he had it when driving the Valiant. Life does teach us some major lessons. One night coming home late from work, he wrecked the car. The wreck didn't involve another vehicle. Paul III told us afterwards that an old woman pulled out in front of him right as he was turning a curve and to avoid hitting her, he ran off the road. The car hit a concrete barrier and the wheels stopped, but the car kept going. Jane and I am not sure what really happened. However, his story made us wonder if he was going too fast and lost control in the curve. Only Paul III knows the real story. Another of life's lessons. The cost to repair the car was far greater than it was worth. The car was totaled and he was only able to recoup only a small part of what he had spent fixing up the vehicle.

Paul III had now learned the joy and despair of owning your own car. He started searching for a replacement. He finally found a beautiful emerald green Ford Gran Torino with a Cleveland engine. Now you talk about horsepower and speed. This car was superfast. This taught him additional lessons. If it walks like a duck and talks like a duck, it is a duck. If it looks like it is fast and is fast, it is a ticket. Yes, he got some tickets. He liked driving fast as a young person and still does today. He made an observation that is probably right on target. He drove the Valiant just as fast and on the same roads that he drove the Gran Torino. He never got a ticket. Who would think a Plymouth Valiant was a race car? On the other hand, the Gran Torino looked fast and was fast and the tickets kept coming.

Huntervationist Is a Huntervationist Regardless of the Season

When Paul III was about 15 years old, we were hunting on the Buckhorn Sportsman's Club property. He was on a deer stand near Murder Creek and I was on a stand up the hill from him. About 10 o'clock in the morning, I heard a shot in his general direction. It is always exciting when someone takes a shot on a hunt. I hoped Paul III had bagged a deer. I waited for at least 10 minutes before I started down the hill toward his stand. As I got close, I could see him standing on the side of the creek. He told me that a herd of several deer including a large buck came from his left, but on the other side of Murder Creek. He had taken a shot and it appeared the buck had gone down. Now we needed to cross the creek and look for the deer. Since the creek was fairly wide and deep, we looked for an area where we could best ford to the other side. Once on the other side, we proceeded to look for the deer. In no time at all, we found the deer in the general area where he thought the deer was. However, there was a problem. He had shot a doe, not a buck. To compound the problem, this part of the hunting season was buck only. Paul III asked me what we were going to do. My response was that regardless of the circumstances, we needed to field-dress the deer and take it home to process. We would have normally taken the deer to a meat processor but in this instance, this was not possible. After field-cleaning the deer, we cut down a small sapling and tied the legs of the deer to the new pole and carried the deer to the car Robin Hood style. We were hoping not to be seen by anyone, but especially a game warden. Once at the car, placing the deer in the trunk of the Plymouth Valiant was a challenge. Once this was accomplished, off to home we went.

When we got home, I had Jane open the basement door. After placing a tarpaulin on the basement floor, the two hunters hauled the deer inside and placed it on the floor. The rest of the story will not be described in detail. The fact that I had not ever processed a deer and did not have the right tools will tell you something. It was like something from a murder scene. It was a horrific mess. However, we did harvest some nice cuts of meat. I was able to ground some of meat into venison burgers. However, I learned quickly, this was the first and last time that I would ever process a deer. After butchering the deer and I do mean butchering it, we took the carcass to the high school and put it into a dumpster. The whole time we were hoping that no one would see us. Thank goodness cameras were not commonly used during this era.

The moral of the story is that Paul III learned when we kill one of God's creations, a good hunter makes sure the meat is eaten by someone. In other words, a huntervationist is a huntervationist, no matter what.

Miss Him Once, Miss Him Twice

My son, Paul III, started hunting with me when he was a young teenager. From the beginning, it was obvious that he learned quickly. His ability with a rifle was in a class by itself. Only one other person that I ever hunted with was close to being his equal and that was a friend of mine, Jim Blair. Jim invited members of the Buckhorn Sportsman's Club to his country home in Griffin, Georgia, every year to sight-in their weapons. This was always done prior to deer season so that people could make sure their rifles were on target. These gatherings became competitive events after a while for members to demonstrate their shooting skills. This is where I learned what a great shot Jim was. Over time, Paul III was involved and as his shooting skills were refined, it was clear he was a superior rifleman. In the military he would have been called an expert.

The above is a precursor to demonstrate that if your scope is not on target, you will not hit what you are aiming for. On one of our hunting trips, Paul III and I were hunting about a 100-yards from each other. He was on a stand where many deer had been harvested over time. After about an hour I heard a shot in his general direction. Shortly, I heard a second shot. This was highly unusual, as normally if he shot, it was a kill. Several minutes later, there was a third shot. It is a standard operating practice to wait at least 30 minutes after shooting at a deer before getting off the stand. This makes sure that if the deer is only wounded, it will remain down. In other words, you don't want to spook the deer and have to track it down. After about 30 minutes after the last shot, I walked over to Paul III's stand.

When I got there, he was dejected. He had shot at a large big-tine buck with at least 14 points. He said it was the most magnificent deer he had ever seen on the property. He took careful aim and missed. The buck just stood there looking around so he shot a second time. Again, the deer just stood there and then slowly walked away. A few minutes later a herd of does came into the area and he took careful aim and shot. All the does instantly ran away, including the doe that he shot at. Paul III was dumbfounded. He had done everything right and each shot should have brought down the deer. My advice to him was that something had to be wrong with the scope. I suggested that we go to the place on the property that we used as a shooting range and check out the scope. We did and the result was that he could not hit the target. After several adjustments to the scope, he began to hit dead center on the target. Somehow, the scope had been rattled or bumped and clearly was the reason that he had missed the deer. This experience taught us the importance of checking out your scope routinely. A crack shot is only as good as a sighted-in scope.

As a side story, I remember good times taking target practice with Paul III when he was in his teens. I had bought a stainless Ruger Redhawk .41 magnum pistol. I already had a Ruger Blackhawk .44 magnum pistol that I bought from Don Stenhouse. These two pistols are very powerful weapons. As a result, they have quite a kick when shot. Both are capable of bringing deer down as well as most rifles. Paul III and I would go to a dump that was on our hunting property and practice for hours. One of our favorite shooting scenarios was placing old bottles on the top of old refrigerators. Then using one of the pistols we would shoot at the bottles. We got proficient enough that most times we would hit all the bottles without a miss. Then we started practicing shooting bottles with one of these powerful guns in each hand. We got to the point that we could hit bottles without missing by firing with one gun in the right hand and one gun in the left hand. To be truthful, I was very impressed that we could do that. One thing became very clear that Paul III's hand and eye coordination was extraordinary. He can hit whatever he shoots at with rifle and pistol.

Stronger Than Most Bears

Paul III, my son, was hunting with Don Stenhouse, Joe McGee, and me at the Due West Hunting Club property near Washington, Georgia. The hunting property had more deer harvested annually than anywhere I had ever hunted in Georgia. Many of the deer harvested were by our party of hunters. Don, Joe, and I enjoyed hunting with Little Paul as we called Paul III. He had been hunting with us since he was a pup. Little Paul was in his early twenties, almost six-feet-two inches tall, and weighed about 220 pounds. Needless to say, he literally looked down on his three elders.

On this morning hunt, we all occupied deer stands in an area that was one of our favorites. Many deer had been successfully taken in this area. It was a cold morning and it was especially cold when we each went to our stands before daybreak. As the sun slowly rose in the east, the woods became alive with sound. It is always one of the most beautiful and exciting times of a morning hunt. About midmorning a shot rang out in the direction where Paul III was hunting. After waiting for close to an hour, I came out of the woods onto an old logging road. Then I proceeded in the direction where Paul III was hunting. When I got to the end of the road, Don and Joe were already there. Where the road ended was a very steep incline to an open bottom. This was where Paul III's stand was. We all decided to stay where we were for two reasons. We didn't want to bother him if he was still hunting. It was also obvious the rugged hill would not have been very much fun to walk down and climb back up.

The three of us talked, waited, and tried to keep warm. After some time, we heard noise and assumed it was Paul III. As he climbed the hill, we were dumbfounded at what we saw. Rather than dragging the deer, he had the deer on his shoulders carrying it up the hill. This was not a small deer, but a full-grown deer. To add to the weight, it had not yet been field- dressed. He had manhandled the deer and carried it several hundred yards including up the hill. As a former football player, we knew he was strong. However, none of us realized that he was as strong as a bear.

B. Robert
Reading at Two?

When we were living in Mississippi, I came home from work one afternoon and Jane said your son has something to show you. Robert was in the bathroom sitting on the toilet seat. Jane handed a book, a primer, and asked him to read. He started to read and after several pages it was obvious that he could read as well as most first graders. Shockingly, he was barely over two years old. Thinking back, we probably could contribute this phenomenon to several things. One, he was very smart. To confirm this assertion, he was in advanced courses from elementary school through high school. When he graduated from high school, because of joint college enrollment, he had already completed three-quarters of his freshman year of college. Further, he graduated among the top in his class and received numerous college scholarships including from Ivy League Schools. Secondly, he benefited from television shows like *Sesame Street* and *The Electric Company*. He absorbed information from these shows and they really made a difference in his education and advancement. Thirdly, Jane and I routinely read, especially his mother who he idolized. Last, his older brother, Paul III, was a great role model and set a high standard for him. He read early, but he had a great deal of positive things going for him.

Should Have Been City Champion

When we lived in Austin, our subdivision, Balcones Woods, had a swimming team. The team competed with other swimming teams from all over metropolitan Austin. The swimming coach had tryouts to determine who would compete in each event. Both Paul III and Robert were very good swimmers and were selected to swim in several events. Against other swimming clubs they were both unbeatable in their age class. Paul III's best event was the backstroke. I don't believe he was ever beaten in head-to-head competition in this event. Suffice it to say he won a lot of blue ribbons and gold medals for first place. The same is true for Robert. He won many gold medals and blue ribbons in several different events. However, in the breaststroke Robert was in a class by himself.

During the year he set records in the breaststroke. No one ever came close to beating him. Robert's style was to swim just as fast as he needed to swim to win. The better the competition the faster he would swim. At the end of the year, the best swimmers from all over the city were selected to compete for the Austin championship. As usual Robert won heat after heat and advanced to the finals. The difference this time was because of the number of swimmers to compete in the finals, there would be two heats not one. The fastest time would be crowned city champion. Robert as usual won his heat by a large margin. In the second heat a swimmer that Robert had already beaten twice early in the year won the second heat. Now came the backbreaker. The other swimmer won by a faster time. Robert because of his time finished second. There was no doubt in anyone's mind that was in the know that during a head-to-head competition, Robert would have beaten the other swimmer. Remember, Robert would go just fast enough to win. Jane and I were happy with his performance, but disappointed in the outcome. Robert should have been Austin city champion.

Involvement with Our Sons

While Jane and I lived in Austin, we spent a lot of time with our sons, Paul III and Robert. Since we agreed that Jane wouldn't work, she was the main parent during the day every week. Since both boys were involved in a great many activities such as sports, scouts, swimming, and school affairs, she was kept busy chauffeuring them around northwest Austin. At night and weekends, I was deeply involved with them concerning sports, scouts, and Indian Y-Guides.

Robert was involved in the Indian Y-Guides. I remember that we wore headbands with feathers and a decorative yellow and red vest with different native American symbols. We met every couple of weeks at different members' homes. We had a guidebook and did various projects. The main mission of the program was to instill camaraderie between father and son. I remember attending jamborees that invited competition between tribes. This is when I began to learn how agile Robert was. I remember one event that featured a large rope hanging from the ceiling. Each brave was challenged to climb the rope as far as they could toward what appeared to be a 15 foot plus ceiling. Most braves didn't get very far off the ground. A few were able to climb halfway to the top. When it was Robert's turn, he climbed to the top like a monkey. His agility was remarkable. At that age I wouldn't have gotten very far. The Indian Y-Guides program was very good for both of us and I really believe it sealed a closer bond between us. This bond would last for the rest of his life. However, the bond between Jane and Robert was even stronger.

Cub Scouts was another activity that Robert and I enjoyed together. We did the usual things that scouts do. We learned how to make things and enjoyed many fun projects and activities. The two activities I enjoyed most were the Pinewood Derby and the camping at the Bastrop Boy Scout facility when he was a Webelo. The Pinewood Derby required each Cub Scout to design a wooden racer from a block of wood. You had to add wheels to the frame. Parents could help. In truth some parents did all the work. All racers had to meet weight limits and other stringent requirements. The pack would develop an elevated racetrack that again had to meet designated standards. I remember another CDC public health advisor assignee to Texas, Gene Williams, and our boys building our racers at his house. I believe Gene also built the pack's racetrack. We designed our cars, shaped our cars, sanded our cars, painted our cars, weighed out cars, and in essence did everything to get our cars ready. We learned that the heavier the racer, the faster it would run. It was permissible to add weight like lead. I decided rather than using lead, I would add two silver dollars to Robert's racer. This made his car very unique. If a car was too heavy, it would be disqualified. Therefore, it was necessary to get the weight just right. Since Gene had built the racetrack for the pack and it was at his house, we had fun testing our cars and improving their performance. Gene's son, Beau's, car would win. Then Robert's car would win.

On race day, each den member would compete with the fastest two cars being designated den winners. Then they would compete against other den winners. The fastest two racers would represent the pack and compete against other pack winners. Robert and Gene's son, Beau, finished one and two in the den competition. I believe Beau's racer was first. In the pack races Robert and Beau finished first and second again. I really don't know which car was fastest, but they were always neck and neck. The bottom line is how much fun Gene and I had with our sons. At the end of the day that was what it was all about. In retrospect, without question, had Robert and I not had the help of Gene's mechanical skills, we probably wouldn't have been as competitive.

Camping at the Bastrop Boy Scout Camp was Robert's first real taste of camping outdoors. He enjoyed the beauty and the fresh air. He enjoyed the structured life. He enjoyed being able to hike and romp and stomp. Robert never became the outdoors man that his brother, Paul III, and I did. For me, I just enjoyed being with my son.

Stitch Me Up Once, Stitch Me Up Twice

Robert was a very active child and that by no means is an overstatement. If Paul III was quiet, Jane was not ever worried. He was basically very well behaved. On the other hand, if Robert was quiet, she would go looking for him. Part of Robert's problem was that he was very inquisitive and the other was that he was a risk taker. Paul III used to say if Robert had been born first, he would not have been born. He may have been right.

When we lived in Mississippi, I was away hunting for the day. I returned home to find Robert with a large patch on his forehead. Jane explained what had happened. Robert had his brother's Superman outfit on and decided to test his flying ability. He climbed up on the chest of drawers and leaped for the bed. He missed the mattress and hit the bed and split his head open. After Jane got the bleeding stopped with a clean towel, she called her friend, Carol Taute, who had a second car. Carol took her to our doctor who took one look and referred Jane to a plastic surgeon. Several layers of very fine stiches fixed the problem. After a period of time, Robert showed no noticeable scar. The plastic surgeon was the right call.

On another occasion when we lived in Stone Mountain, Robert had another major accident. While Jane's mother, Lavinia Corley Miller, was visiting, Robert was riding his bicycle up and down the hill in front of our house. The children in the neighborhood loved riding down the hill because they were able to pick up a great deal of speed. On one of the times, he was coming down the hill at a fast pace, his shoelace got caught in the gears of the bicycle. As he attempted to remove the string, he took his eyes off the road. He ran straight into a mailbox. For the second time he had split his head wide open. After hearing about the accident, Jane, her mother, and I ran to where he was lying. With towels in hand, we stopped the bleeding and evaluated the wound. It was long and deep. There was no question that Robert needed stitches. Jane from her previous experience knew he needed a plastic surgeon. After calling our family physician, he referred us to what he considered the best plastic surgeon in Atlanta. On calling the doctor, he was able to see Robert immediately. The surgeon used 25 stitches in three layers to fix the wound. That is right, 75 carefully placed stitches. One deep-set, one intermediary-set, and another set on the surface. He explained this would prevent a scar and the procedure would enhance healing and durability. He was right, Robert had no scar and the only time you would notice the area above his eye was when he had been in the sun.

Robert's love for life and his aggressive nature served him well, but there were some bumps along the way.

The Refereed Fight

Robert, Jane and my youngest son, was active, athletic, and not scared of anything. He was sometimes too smart for his own good. When we lived in Stone Mountain, there was a boy that lived down the street named Tim Snyder. Tim was a couple of years older than Robert and much bigger. For some reason they just didn't get along. Routinely, when they were around each other, there were words exchanged and some pushing and shoving. The intensity of their encounters increased over time. Several neighborhood children were in our Stone Mountain neighborhood yard, including Tim. Jane observed out the window that the next conflict of these two was beginning to occur. Jane had had enough. She went into the yard and summoned both Robert and Tim over to where she stood. She told them if they were going to fight each other, she would be the referee. It would be a fair fight and that they could end the hostility toward each other once and for all.

With Jane as the referee, the boys pushed and shoved each other. Eventually, a few punches were thrown. Then more punches were thrown. Each was giving as much as they received. After several minutes the fight was over. There was no clear winner. Both boys shook hands and agreed that whatever disagreement that they had, was now settled. Eventually, they began to respect each other, although they never became close friends. In fact, they played football together at Stone Mountain High School.

Jane would have never allowed either boy to be seriously hurt. Her unorthodox method to settle their grievance had worked. The growing tension had been defused. The neighborhood was a better place because of her efforts. In today's culture, Jane's decision to referee and to settle the matter would probably be scorned by some.

Somebody Needed Help, but It Wasn't Robert

When Paul III was in high school, his brother, Robert, was in the eighth grade. They both played football. One was on the varsity and the other was on the B team. Paul III was at football practice when a friend came up to him and stated that a gang of 10th graders were attacking Robert and his friend, Steven Downey. Paul III went to his head coach, Tom Van Tone, and asked permission to go help his brother. After receiving permission, he went to find his brother. As he became close to where he thought Robert was, he saw that one 10th grader was down and out of the fight. Soon he saw another and then another. They had been whipped and licking their wounds. Robert has taken out three older and bigger boys. His friend had taken out the other. This gang of supposed toughs had learned the hard way, you don't mess with Robert. Somebody needed help, but it wasn't Robert.

Paul III asked Robert what had happened. For some unexplained reason, the four 10th graders confronted Robert and Steve in a menacing way. The biggest and the leader of the toughs aggressively approached Robert and before he knew it, Robert struck first. The largest guy was now down and out, now the rest were not so tough. The rest were put down by the two friends. All is well that ends well. Unneeded, Paul III went back to practice.

Close, but No Cigar

Robert, our youngest son, played football and wrestled in high school. He was a starting football guard in the 10th grade. Although smaller than most linemen, he was aggressive and quick. With all that said, he really liked wrestling best. In his senior year, he gave up football to concentrate on wrestling. There were three reasons for his decision. The first was the head football coach left and Robert didn't want to have to prove himself all over again to the new coach. Second, he was tired of having to gain weight for football and then lose weight for wrestling. Third, he was captain of the wrestling team and wanted to give it his full attention.

With that all said, during his senior year, the Stone Mountain wrestling team was very good. Robert and his coach made a good team. His coach put wrestlers into weight classes that would make them more competitive. Stone Mountain won most of their matches and several wrestlers, including Robert, qualified for the Georgia state competition. In Robert's heat, there were several very good wrestlers including the reigning state champion. Robert was able to win his first matches fairly easily. In the quarter finals, he would face the state champion from the year before. In each match, there are three rounds. In the first two rounds both wrestlers were even in points. Neither has come close to being pinned. With a pin the match is over. In the third round, the champion was ahead by one point with one minute left in the match. Robert's favorite wrestling move was the Peterson. Once you are in the Peterson, the opponent's arms and legs are locked in a manner that the person is pinned and the match is over. Robert started to make his move and maneuvered the champion into the Peterson. With seconds left in the match, Robert had the champion in the Peterson. The match would be his. Unfortunately, time ran out. One more second and he would have won the match and probably would have been the state champion. He had come close, but no cigar. It is worth noting that Robert was never pinned in his long high school wrestling career.

Everybody Is on Their Own

Robert was on the student counsel the five years that he was at Stone Mountain High School. He was president of the student body his senior year. Key leaders were sent each year for a student council retreat to Rock Eagle, an FFA camp near Madison, Georgia. The camp is on a beautiful lake and the grounds are significant and pristine. An ideal place for a retreat. Representatives came from schools from all across the area. Robert loved to have fun and if a prank was being developed, he would be at the center of the activity.

Since it was close to Halloween, a prank was developed to scare some of the other campers. Robert had borrowed his brother Paul III's favorite Halloween mask, a realistic werewolf head, and brought it with him to the retreat. There was a long bridge that crossed over a significant branch that fed into the lake. Once across the bridge, there was an open area and then the lake. In other words, you were on an island. Several feet from the bridge on the lake side was a large tree. Robert's plan was to climb the tree and then place the mask on. The first group to pass under the tree would receive the full impact of his devised terror. Near dusk, he climbed the tree, sat on a lower limb, and arranged the mask in the right position. Then he waited. Shortly, a group of black males and females from Atlanta came across the bridge. It was obvious that some of the males were enamored with some of the females and were trying to be impressive. As soon as they passed the tree, Robert leaped down and as he hit the ground, he made a loud roar. One look at the werewolf, the group of several ran in every direction. There was no chivalry among the young men, the girls were on their own. Robert had scared them into a total hysteria. Some ran through the branch to get to the other side. Other members got as far away as they could from the bridge. In all the confusion, Robert creeped back to the camp. The werewolf was the talk of the retreat. No one knew where it had come from and where it went. Robert and his friends knew, but they were not going to tell.

What Is Going to Happen at Graduation?

Robert graduated from Stone Mountain High School in 1987. As he was president of the student body, he was heavily involved in the graduation ceremony. He was to give a commencement speech and present several awards. He was also to receive some awards. His class knew from experience that he was going to do something unorthodox and humorous. The principal also knew the potential for Robert to do something off the wall and warned him beforehand to stay within the graduation boundaries. This was based on some of the things he had done as student body president. With the assistant principal, Scott Butler's blessings, one time, Robert wore his pajamas and animal slippers to school. Of course, this provided humor to school life and later led to a day when the whole student body was allowed to do the same. On another occasion, he talked the administration into allowing the whole student body to use roller skates between classes. In other words, Robert had the reputation of making serious endeavors fun.

Prior to graduation, he had his mother take some dress pants and cut the legs off near the knees. Then the bottom parts of the pant legs were attached back with Velcro. With a slight pull, dress pants would become Bermuda shorts. On the afternoon of graduation, he dressed with shirt, tie, and modified dress pants. Then he put on his gown and cap.

Our family watched as the graduation ceremony went along smoothly. Robert did a wonderful job on his parts during the program and we were thrilled with the different recognitions he received. Then came the part where diplomas were presented by the principal. The diplomas were presented in alphabetical order and therefore Robert was near the last. As he received his diploma, the whole class cheered. Once past the principal, he raised his gown and ripped the pants legs off. The class howled in excitement with some throwing their caps in the air prematurely. Robert had not disappointed his class and had met their expectations.

Grandchildren and Great-Grandchildren

Over the years, we have stories that concern Jane and my parents, Jane's siblings and their families. This section features our grandchildren and now our great-grandchildren. This section includes these stories.

A. Grandchildren
The State Park That Was a Treasure

When we lived in Stone Mountain the nearby Stone Mountain State Park was a regular attraction for our family. There were numerous things to enjoy. I think the most significant were: The Confederate Memorial featuring Robert E. Lee, Stonewall Jackson, and Jefferson Davis; the War in Georgia Museum; the antebellum planation; the tram to the top of Stone Mountain; the beautiful seasonal Christmas decorations which were in a class by themselves; and the hiking trails to the summit. Our sons, Paul III and Robert, enjoyed routine trips to Stone Mountain for picnics, concerts, Easter Sunrise services, hiking, fishing, etc. when they were growing up. As high schoolers they enjoyed going there with friends and dates. Stone Mountain was without question a major resource for the Turner family. Family and friends who came for a visit were treated to trips to the park with all of its attractions.

Therefore, it is not surprising that as our sons got married and had families, Stone Mountain Park still took center stage when we were entertaining our grandchildren, Andrew, Amanda, and Stephanie. At Christmas, the Stone Mountain Park was amazing. There were a plethora of Christmas decorations including decorated cards, various vehicles covered in lights, the blinking lights strung on lines between poles, trees that were ornate, and the centerpiece being the regally decorated antebellum planation. Our grandchildren's expressions of awe and delight made all of us adults truly happy with the Christmas spirit. Over time all three, Andrew, Amanda, and Stephanie, participated in virtually all of Stone Mountain Park's venues and opportunities. Christmas, Easter, and the summer concerts and light shows in front of the Confederate Memorial (Sculpture) were my personal favorites.

I think the Christmas experience was probably my grandchildren's favorite from a very young age. I know that one of Andrew's most favorite experience was riding ponies that were named after the Little Rascals. I remember Darla, Froggy, Alfalfa, and Spanky. Once he found the pony ride, it became a routine on any park visit.

I haven't been to Stone Mountain Park for years. However, I remember fondly how many good times our family had there. Stone Mountain State Park was truly a treasure to the whole Turner clan.

I Didn't Touch It

When our grandson, Andrew, was in an Atlanta nursery, he was being taught personal hygiene. Jane and I were reinforcing good behavior when he stayed with us. One good habit that he was being taught was to always wash your hands after going to the bathroom. Every time he went to the bathroom, one of us would always remind him to wash his hands. Our goal was that over time he would instinctively wash his hands. One day, Andrew and I were in a public restroom together and were both using the toilet. Andrew finished first and was heading out the door without washing his hands. He saw me watching him and without breaking stride he said, "I didn't touch it." This young child had figured out that if he didn't touch his tee-tee bug, it was not necessary to wash his hands.

Another side story is about Andrew and having to urinate. I have never seen a child that very seldom had to relieve himself. He certainly didn't inherit his bladder from me. He had to have one large and magnificent bladder. After what seemed forever, he would say I have to go. It was no question that he was now ready and there would be no delay. One day we were driving home in heavy traffic and Andrew told his Mimi that he had to go tee-tee. We started looking for any facility with a restroom to no avail. With urgency he said I have to go bad. I pulled over at a bank. Jane took him into the shrubbery lining the bank so that he could relieve himself. This was done with numerous cars zooming by. In other words, I have to go means, I have to go right now.

Jaws in a Pond

When we lived in Cumming, we went to church with Greer and Judy Austin. The Austin family lived on a compound with his father and mother near the subdivision where we lived. It was beautiful land with a lot of acreage. On the land was a very large farm pond. Greer allowed my grandson, Andrew, and I to fish the pond. We would always call ahead and, if it suited, we would drive the mile or so to the pond. We did this on a regular basis. We caught a number of fish and for the most part we caught the fish and then we released them. In other words, we just enjoyed being together and having fun. I really enjoyed teaching Andrew how to fish and seeing him mature in his fishing skills. He was becoming a very good fisherman. He was doing everything right every time.

One day, we were fishing around the edge of the pond and making our way to a wooden pier. We caught bream on the way. We caught a few nice fish and as usual released them. Once we got to the pier, we began casting to various locations to find where a fish might be residing. On one of Andrew's cast, he hooked a very nice large-mouth bass that weighed about two pounds. He started to reel it in. He kept the line tight as he had been taught and was making good progress in bringing his catch in. As the fish was next to the pier, we saw an amazing occurrence. A very large-mouth bass was coming in fast behind the fish that Andrew had caught. The bass I estimated to weigh at least 12 pounds. It was humongous. The large bass's mouth opened looking like the Great White shark in *Jaws*. It gained speed and then it looked like it had inhaled the two-pound bass. Now it looked like Andrew had a chance to catch the biggest bass I had ever seen. I instructed him not to place tension on the line and let the large bass go wherever it wanted to go. With four-pound test line the only chance to catch this mammoth was to wear him out. Andrew would have to reel him in slowly and then when he would bolt, release the tension. The fight was on between fisherman and fish. Every time we thought the bass was worn-out, he would take off again. After several minutes, the monster finally broke the line. Andrew had done well, but the large-mouth bass had won his freedom and would live another day. What fun Andrew and I had had. All we could think about was what could have been.

Break the Rules, Pay the Price

When Andrew was about seven years old, I bought a BB gun so that I could teach him how to properly handle a firearm. I wanted him to learn how to safely shoot. There were several reasons for doing this at his young age. One, I am a hunter and a shooter and as result I have a number of pistols and long guns in my homes. Secondly, I wanted to teach him that every firearm is to be considered loaded and handled accordingly. Third, I wanted him to learn to shoot correctly so that he could be proficient and a marksman. Lastly, I wanted him to enjoy firearms and the sportsmanship surrounding the use of various weapons. I felt fully qualified to accomplish the above tasks as at one time

I was a certified National Rifle Association safe shooting instructor. As a Jaycee I had instructed hundreds of young people how to safely shoot.

I initially taught Andrew how to safely handle a BB gun. Then I taught him how to safely load the weapon. He was then taught how to properly aim and shoot. After practicing aiming at a target, he was allowed to shoot at a target. He was able to master all phases of the training. He became a good shot and practiced safe procedures. I was very proud of him. My final instruction was for him to never handle the BB gun or any of my weapons unless I was with him.

One day, we were enjoying shooting when I had to go into the house for a few minutes. When I returned, Andrew was not only shooting without me being present, but shooting at one of my bird feeders. I took the gun from him and scolded him for violating my rules. His punishment was to go to his room and lose his shooting privileges for a specified period of time. He stomped off and went to his room. It was one of the few times I saw him mad. I believe he was as mad at himself as he was at me. He knew he had disappointed me. His Mimi, Jane, talked to him and told him he needed to apologize to me. I was resting in my recliner when Andrew's bedroom door opened. He came to me with tears in his eyes, climbed into my lap, hugged my neck, and apologized to me. I believed he learned a good lesson.

Shooting Is a Turner Family Affair

I had been a hunter even before I was a teenager. I learned to enjoy taking target practice with various firearms. As a result, I taught my sons, Paul III and Robert, how to shoot properly and the art of hunting. Paul III excelled at both. Robert excelled at shooting and became a marksman in the Army ROTC at Mercer University. Robert never really enjoyed hunting. Probably because he never had the patience it took to hunt. However, he did become a good fisherman. Therefore, it became natural for my grandchildren to learn how to shoot at a young age. Not only are they good shots, they each have weapons for self-defense. In this day and time, it is not only important to legally carry a weapon, but to know how and when to shoot.

When my son, Paul III, and his wife, Kathy, along with my granddaughters, Amanda, Kelly, and Stephanie, would come to the mountains to see us, most of the time, we at some point would go somewhere to shoot. Initially, we shot BB guns, .22 rifles, and pellet guns, and eventually we shot higher-caliber weapons. Paul III would bring an assortment of targets and of course I had targets too. We would set up targets and take turns shooting. At times we would shoot for quite some time. We always enjoyed these outings. Amanda, Kelly, and Stephanie became very good shots. Paul III had taught them well.

Over Thanksgiving and Christmas, Paul III, my grandson, Andrew, and I would shoot competitively and try to outshoot each other. We all three are good shots, but Paul III is the best. Shooting and firearms have always been a constant in our family. We love shooting, hunting, and the outdoors.

Who IS in Control?

My granddaughters, Amanda and Stephanie's mother, Sally Johnson Turner, is an equestrian. She has trained and shown horses and ponies since she was a child. She has been involved in horse shows all over the southeastern United States and has won hundreds of ribbons. One of her horses was a world champion. Amanda and Stephanie were involved while their mother trained and showed horses from the time that they were tots. At this point, I would like to point out this is a very expensive sport. The animals are expensive as well as their upkeep, their training, their transporting to shows, stable fees, cost of forage, etc. Most awards are ribbons not money. Therefore, it is not surprising that they were encouraged to become involved in the sport. Amanda of the two girls began to learn the skills required of an equestrian. She started to practice and participate in shows.

Jane and I often attended the different horseshows in which Sally was involved. Therefore, it should be no surprise that we would be in attendance when Amanda would take centerstage. Sally, as she got older principally showed a Hackney pony, Linebacker, who was a World champion. She would be pulled in a cart and Sally would guide him through the performance. By the way, I know it is not a cart and not a chariot, but I do not remember the technical name. Amanda's horse, Beau, was a very well-built large animal. The first time I saw my small granddaughter on this large animal, my thoughts were how can she control this horse? In other words, who is in control? I found out quickly that Amanda was in control. She walked Beau through his routine and over time she begun to win ribbons. Sally had trained Amanda well. To this day I can see my small and petite granddaughter on Beau.

After a period of time competing, Amanda grew tired of the long hour of training her horse and perfecting her skills. As she grew older, her interest went elsewhere.

We Want Proof of That Girl's Age

Paul III for a few years coached his three girls, Kelly, Amanda, and Stephanie, in basketball. All three girls were on the same team in a very competitive league in Gwinnet County, Georgia. Jane and I on occasion would go to their games to watch our three granddaughters play and, of course, watch Paul III coach. We were delighted to watch their games and found them to be very competitive. Each girl brought their own set of skills to the game. Kelly was about average size and was a good shooter, but really excelled on defense. Amanda was shortest of the three, but was an effective guard who was fast and could handle the ball well. Stephanie, although the youngest of the three, was tall and the best athlete. She would dominate the game under the basket. Her shooting and rebounding carried the team. She had ability way beyond her years. In fact, one coach had the commissioner of the league look at her birth certificate to prove her age.

The team won many games in the league. The wins were the result of two things. Paul III's exquisite coaching and the play of the three girls. Each game we attended was exciting. To see our three granddaughters playing on the same team and our son coaching was wonderful.

Because of Stephanie's height and natural and superior ability, the family could see her doing well in high school basketball, and we all envisioned the potential for a future college scholarship. However, Stephanie was not inclined to play sports in high school.

B. Great-Grandchildren
Charlotte Jean

On April 20, 2016 my granddaughter, Stephanie Turner, gave birth to a beautiful baby girl, Charlotte Jean. With her birth the Turner family had its fourth living generation. Our lives would be changed forever. Paul III was now a grandparent. From the start Charlotte was very active. She is beautiful and it is obvious that she is very smart. In addition to that she is going to be tall like her mother and daddy and is very coordinated (athletic). I bet this appears that a proud great-grandfather is just bragging. Nope, not at all, this is a factual evaluation about my great-granddaughter. She is special in every way.

After her birth she has been the center of attention at most Turner family gatherings. The exception is when her cousin, Atlas, is visiting from Philadelphia. Then they both receive a lot of attention. I do know that if Jane and I want any quality time with her, it must be before the rest of the family arrives. Thank goodness, Paul III and his wife, Kathy, make that happen often. Once the family gets there, Charlotte is all over the place. Of all the people outside her mother and father, John McLean, the people she has bonded with the most are Kathy and her Aunt Amanda's husband, Joe Norton. What is amazing about this love, is that neither Kathy or Joe has her DNA. This illustrates that love has nothing to with heredity. Charlotte has changed our lives forever. She is without question a wonderful gift from God.

Atlas Grey

On October 23, 2018 our granddaughter, Kelly Pensmith, gave birth to a handsome young man, Atlas Grey. He is beautiful too, but boys are not called beautiful. Atlas is not going be as big as his cousin Charlotte, but I am sure he will also be smart, athletic, and active. The family enjoys being with Atlas when he visits Paul III and Kathy from Philadelphia. There is no doubt when he visits with the Turner family, his Nana, Kathy, and his cousin, Charlotte, give him the most attention. The attention of both is constantly on Atlas. As he gets to know the family more, there will be more bonding. It will be fun seeing him grow up.

With the arrival of Charlotte and Atlas, the family is growing in many ways. Through the eyes of these two sweet children, the family is being reconnected to many joys that we once knew, but have forgotten. To see the world through the eyes of a child is wonderful and fulfilling. I hope to live long enough to see them mature into young adults. Through these two precious creatures the Turner family moves forward, at least our DNA does.

Lightning Source UK Ltd.
Milton Keynes UK
UKHW020752250821
389444UK00015B/1005